Teaching and Program Variations in International Business

Teaching and Program Variations in International Business has been co-published simultaneously as *Journal of Teaching in International Business*, Volume 10, Numbers 3/4 1999.

Teaching and Program Variations in International Business

Erdener Kaynak, PhD, DSc
John R. Schermerhorn, Jr., PhD
Editors

Teaching and Program Variations in International Business has been co-published simultaneously as *Journal of Teaching in International Business*, Volume 10, Numbers 3/4 1999.

Routledge
Taylor & Francis Group
NEW YORK AND LONDON

First published 1999 by The Haworth Press, Inc.

Published 2021 by Routledge
605 Third Avenue, New York, NY 10017
2 Park Square, Milton Park, Abingdon, Oxon OX14 4RN

First issued in paperback 2021

Routledge is an imprint of the Taylor & Francis Group, an informa business

Teaching and Program Variations in International Business has been co-published simultaneously as *Journal of Teaching in International Business,* Volume 10, Numbers 3/4 1999

Notice:
Product or corporate names may be trademarks or registered trademarks and are used only for identification and explanation without intent to infringe.

Publisher's Note
The publisher has gone to great lengths to ensure the quality of this reprint but points out that some imperfections in the original copies may be apparent.

Cover design by Thomas J. Mayshock Jr.

Library of Congress Cataloging-in-Publication Data

Teaching and program variations in international business/Erdener Kaynak, John R. Schermerhorn, Jr. editors.

p. cm.

"Teaching and program variations in international business has been co-published simultaneously as Journal of teaching in international business, vol. 10, numbers 3/4 1999."

Includes bibliographical references and index.

ISBN 0-7890-0809-2 (alk. paper)

1. International business enterprises–Management–Study and teaching. 2. Business education–International cooperation. I. Kaynak, Erdener. II. Schermerhorn, John R., Jr.

HD62.4 .T4 1999
658′.049′071–dc21 99-056468

ISBN 13: 978-1-138-99677-9 (pbk)
ISBN 13: 978-0-7890-0809-1 (hbk)
ISBN 13: 978-1-315-86226-2 (ebk)

DOI: 10.4324/9781315862262

Teaching and Program Variations in International Business

CONTENTS

ABOUT THE EDITORS

Erdener Kaynak, PhD, DSc, is currently Professor of Marketing and Chair of the Marketing Program at the School of Business Administration of the Pennsylvania State University at Harrisburg. He holds a BEcon degree from Istanbul University, an MA in Marketing from the University of Lancaster and a PhD in Marketing Management from Cranfield University in the United Kingdom, and an honorary DSc degree in Economics from Turku School of Economics and Business Administration, Finland. He has extensive teaching, research, consulting, and advising experiences in five continents and over thirty countries. A prolific writer, Dr. Kaynak has published 22 books, two of which were translated into Japanese and Chinese, and over 200 articles in refereed scholarly and professional journals on international marketing, cross-national/cultural consumer behavior and comparative marketing systems.

He served as a member of the Kyrgyz President's Task Force on Science and Education and has been heavily involved in the development and improvement of the first Western style Business School in Kyrgyz Republic–Bishek International Academy of Business and Management (BIABM) for the last five years. A frequent contributor to executive training programs around the globe, Dr. Kaynak has recently offered seminars before senior executives and public policy makers in such countries as Colombia, Peru, Canada, Finland, Norway, Estonia, Turkey, Italy, Hong Kong, Australia, South Africa, The People's Republic of China, Kyrgyz Republic, The Sudan, Macau, Egypt, Sweden, Germany, Japan, Australia, Denmark and Thailand. Dr. Kaynak has also served as a business consultant, training advisor, and a seminar leader with a number of North/South American, European, and Asian companies and institutions. For the last twelve years, Dr. Kaynak has been serving as the Executive Editor for International Business Press (IBP) as well as the Senior Editor (International Business) for the Haworth Press Inc., of New York, London, and Oxford. In this capacity, he serves as Founding Editor and Editor-in-Chief of six scholarly international marketing and business journals.

Dr. Kaynak has contributed articles to such scholarly publications as *Journal of Advertising Research*, *Journal of the Academy of Marketing Science*, *Journal of Business Research*, *Management International Review*, *Columbia Journal of World Business*, *International Marketing Review*, *Journal of Macromarketing*, *European Journal of Marketing* and many others. He has also been a regular contributor to *International Journal of Advertising*.

John R. Schermerhorn, Jr., PhD, is the O'Bleness Professor of Management in the College of Business and Director of the Center for Southeast Asian Studies at Ohio University. Dr. Schermerhorn received his PhD from Northwestern University. His articles have appeared in the *Academy of Management Journal, Academy of Management Review, Academy of Management Executive,* and *Organizational Dynamics,* among other scholarly and professional journals. The author of *Management,* Sixth Edition (Wiley, 1999) and senior co-author of *Organizational Behavior,* Sixth Edition (Wiley, 1997), he received the University Professor award at Ohio University for excellence in undergraduate teaching. He has worked extensively in Asia as an educator, researcher and consultant, and has further experience in the Middle East, Europe, and Latin America.

Teaching and Program Variations in International Business: Past, Present and Future

Erdener Kaynak
John R. Schermerhorn, Jr.

Over the last three decades, the global economy has changed substantially. This rapid transformation has created enormous market opportunities for firms of all sizes in the trade of physical goods and services. This trend will continue at an accelerating rate as we enter the 21st century. As relationships within and among major trading blocs (North America Free Trade Area–NAFTA, The European Union–EU, and Asia-Pacific Economic Council–APEC will further consolidate. Firms of all sizes and from different regions and countries more than ever before will have to adjust to changing local, national, and international circumstances if they are to be competitive in globalizing world markets.

Within this context, higher education, like any other service industry, is in a state of rapid development, transformation and change in every important respect. One can not, individually or institutionally, count on past accomplishments to deliver future success. The pressures of a complex and ever-changing global environment demand rapid and continuous change and innovation in business education. At present, there is a keen competition among universities all around the world and it is intensifying as they examine their missions and objectives, craft newer business strategies and revise curricula and pedagogies in order to remain vibrant and competitive in today's higher education market. Unrelenting pressures from constituency groups

---

[Haworth co-indexing entry note]: "Teaching and Program Variations in International Business: Past, Present and Future." Kaynak, Erdener and John R. Schermerhorn, Jr. Co-published simultaneously in *Journal of Teaching in International Business* (The International Business Press, an imprint of The Haworth Press, Inc.) Vol. 10, No. 3/4, 1999, pp. 1-10; and: *Teaching and Program Variations in International Business* (ed: Erdener Kaynak and John R. Schermerhorn, Jr.) The International Business Press, an imprint of The Haworth Press, Inc., 1999, pp. 1-10. Single or multiple copies of this article are available for a fee from The Haworth Document Delivery Service [1-800-342-9678, 9:00 a.m.–5:00 p.m. (EST). E-mail address: getinfo@haworthpressinc.com].

and stakeholders alike call for increased relevancy of education to meet the needs of a changing world. Where traditional institutions falter in their market responsiveness, new "corporate" universities are emerging to fill the competitive void all around the world.

All of this unfolds in a global economy characterized by challenges such as changing nature of demand, increased competition, technological advances, governmental interfaces, turmoil, complexity and greater opportunities. The challenge for public and private universities alike is to convert existing threats into lucrative market opportunities by developing need-oriented educational programs and offerings. Importantly, there can be no doubt that the role of international business justifiably stands center stage in the developing agendas of evolving business education.

Those who design and offer international business programs and teach courses must serve as change leaders and integrators as well as motivators. They must be alert for new ways to help close existing performance gaps that leave business graduates with limited global awareness and insufficient cross-cultural sensitivity. And international business educators must do all of this while facing a perplexing and broad-based problem–the fact that most students in our classes, be they graduate or undergraduate, lack first-hand international experience.[1]

Like most problems, however, this one is rich with promising opportunities to be addressed with perseverance, creativity and innovation. This volume describes initiatives that explore new avenues for undergraduate and graduate students to advance their learning about international business, including new forms of alternative pedagogy and new support services.

A number of important themes are interwoven among the papers included in this volume. First, is the real commitment to more "active learning" and "project-based learning," a focus of growing prominence in business education today. This follows the lead of "action learning" which was started in Europe in the early 1960's with the establishment of the world's first Open University. It is linked as well to organizational learning and one of the papers here shows how it applies to international marketing education. It was concluded that the education provided to the students in an international marketing course can be enhanced by focusing on organizational learning tools as a means to increase the shared knowledge level among the students. Second, is the use of advanced computer technologies and programs to facilitate "virtual teamwork," a trend very evident in the emerging workplace in general and in international business in particular. The use of the Internet as a means of communication for teams of students may particularly be useful in this context. This volume describes how virtual team interactions can provide essential experiences of foreign cultures/nations and thought processes, which can be a key component of international business education. Third, is the support services provided to these types of student initiatives. As the accreditation agency American Assembly of Collegiate Schools of business (AACSB) mandates the internationalization of the business curriculum among its member institutions. With culturally-focused (i.e., international marketing) and culturally-enhanced (i.e., cross-cultural communication) courses in place, there is more demand for specialized library and instructional support resources. Fourth, is the reliance on need-oriented programs and courses in international business. How do students feel about international business as a subject area and how should an international component be integrated into existing courses and/or the current business curricula? Hopefully, the papers and the themes presented here will stimulate other international business educators to also report their approaches and share ideas with one another.

The emphasis in active or project-based learning is on engaging students in experiences that require the active application of course ideas or theories (Raelin, 1999). One way to accomplish this in international business education is through some kind of direct field experience. Although there are a variety of forms available–from the traditional semester or year abroad, to summer study programs, to short travel-study visitations (see Kwok, Arpan & Folks, 1994), each is challenged to deliver real increases in global awareness and competency, cultural sensitivity, and international understanding among participating graduate or undergraduate students (Kedia & Cornwell, 1994; Beck, Whiteley & McFetridge, 1996). Simply put, the international field experience is ripe for experimentation, further development and innovation.

In recent years, executive MBA (EMBA) programs at U.S. schools of business have expanded, and international experience has become an integral part of the business curriculum. In many universities, it is a specific four-credit course. In others, it is optional. Regardless of its logistical fit into an EMBA program, this experience must be properly planned and integrated into the overall learning objectives of the entire business program. However, it was found that the experience/course is often planned from a convenience perspective rather than as a strategic part of the curriculum. The paper by Roger Kashlak, Raymond Jones and John Cotner, "Strategically Rethinking the Executive MBA International Business Experience," provides a model for adding strategic rigor when planning and leading a short-term international field experience. Kashlak et al. illustrate the model with a program developed for executive MBAs and requiring an intense period of field work during the academic year. Their program creatively focuses attention on contrasts between developed and emerging country perspectives, as well as industry-level and firm-specific issues. The paper describes how a field experience can and should move beyond "convenience" to be integrated with broader program objectives and implemented with a consequent strategic fit. A series of propositions or guidelines is offered to extend the proposed model for research and practical consideration. The case study application illustrates an international experience that, in addition to front-end activity in the United States, included a 10-day overseas program in Hong Kong, China and Vietnam.

There has been a great deal of discussion among academics as to what is the best approach to "teach" the knowledge and skills that are required for business students to be able to be successful international managers. Most approaches used by business schools to teach international business assist students in developing an awareness of global business issues. However, it is also important to actively move students towards "global competence." Students need to develop skills to be able to learn how to understand and operate effectively in other cultures. Hugh Sherman's paper, "Pursuing Global Competence in an Undergraduate International Business Experience," offers another version of the field study model. Targeted specifically for undergraduate students, his approach involves an intensive summer experience designed with an intricate combination of classroom-based and project activities. The program requires both preparatory academic work prior to departure for the international experience and completion of a real consulting assignment for a local business once in the field. An innovative aspect of this program is that students from Ohio University are joined with students from a local host university on the consulting teams. Sherman believes the consulting teamwork adds directly to the global competencies achieved by student participants.

The Ohio University program described here utilizes a project-based action learning approach to assist undergraduates to learn "global competence." It has four major components and takes place over approximately six weeks during the first of the two summer sessions. The first component of the program takes place on the Ohio University campus. It requires that students learn about concepts concerning international business and to apply these concepts and do further specific research on the country they will visit. Students are required to develop a comprehensive briefing paper as to how a U.S. company conducts business in the country to be visited, e.g., Hungary or Spain. The paper includes a thorough economic, cultural and government profile for possible corporate entry into the country students have chosen.

The second component of this program puts Ohio students into teams with host countries' students to complete a consulting assignment in the host country. The consulting team usually consists of six members, with three from each university. The projects that students work on have been established and agreed upon in advance by the faculty at Ohio University, the faculty of the local Hungarian or Spanish University and the local company representative. The third major component consists of the students traveling around the host country, enjoying the culture. Upon returning home, students are required to complete the fourth major component, which is a 10- to 15-page paper discussing what they learned about cultures, consulting, team work, international business and more.

The author believes that the benefits to the students are substantial. Students gain increased knowledge of local cultures, customers, markets and governments. In addition, they develop critical managerial skills including: (1) greater tolerance of ambiguity; (2) ability to gain multiple perspectives regarding decision-making; and (3) greater ability to work with and manage others. Many of the business students who have participated in this program report that it is one of the (if not the) most rewarding experiences of their entire undergraduate education.

Virtual teamwork is a growing phenomenon in the modern workplace and new groupware technologies makes it increasingly practical (Townsend, De-Marie & Hendrickson, 1998). The paper by David Chappell and John R. Schermerhorn, Jr., "Introducing International Business Experience Through Virtual Teamwork," shows how virtual teamwork can bring the advantages of international business experience into the regular classroom. They describe how term projects in an undergraduate management course can be turned into international business experiences by having students complete them as members of virtual teams. These teams are formed with the assistance of colleagues at universities abroad and work together through electronic computer mediation. Evaluation of the virtual teamwork project shows very positive receptivity by students, as well as an appreciation for the challenges of working together cross–culturally and via computer mediation. The approach offers the potential for low-cost introduction of international business experiences to large numbers of students at the same time that they gain experience with new technologies.

The latter paper fits nicely with one by Don Scott et al., "Crossing the International Teaching Divide–The Evaluation of an Internet Based Teaching Project." Here, Scott et al. detail the results of an investigation into the use of the Internet as a means of communication for teams of students from different universities who were many thousands of miles distant from one another. The aim of the investigation was to identify whether virtual team interactions could produce similar results as face-to-face team interactions.

Teams of students made up from two to three pairs of students from different universities were sent a business project as an assignment. The students interacted by means of the Internet and their project output was evaluated. In addition, the students were surveyed in order to identify their opinions as to the success of the exercise and what modifications could be recommended for the future. Responses were collected in the form of rated responses to closed questions as well as open statements in regard to the students' likes and dislikes in relation to the project and their recommendations for future modifications. The open responses were categorized and the implications of these responses are discussed. The closed questions were used to examine two regression models and to investigate the overall consensus views of the respondents, by examining the mean values of the responses. The result of the investigation has been to show that virtual teams can produce good output and that in the eyes of many of the respondent students, virtual teams can operate as successfully as face-to-face teams.

The implications of the Chappell and Schermerhorn and Scott et al. papers are significant. They suggest that use of the Internet and virtual teams can provide new and very economical ways to link students from different national and cultural backgrounds in shared learning projects. The use of such mixes of people in team interactions can provide essential experience of foreign cultures and thought processes, which is a key component of international business studies today.

The study by G. Thomas Hult and Bruce D. Keillor, "Organizational Learning and Market Orientation in International Marketing Education," focuses on the activities and relationships between the students, faculty, and staff in the international business program. Based on a sample of 193 international marketing students, the results suggest that organizational learning positively affect learning outcomes such as intelligence generation, intelligence dissemination, and responsiveness. The major implication of the study is that the education provided to the students in an international marketing course can be enhanced by focusing on organizational learning tools as a means to increase the shared knowledge level among the students.

Using the organizational learning framework developed by Hult and his colleagues, four distinct but related "orientations" were incorporated into the study of education-related organizational learning and its effect of the three learning outcomes:

- Team orientation is defined as the degree to which educational collaboration and cooperation is present in the learning environment.
- Systems orientation is defined as the degree to which a "broad picture" exists of the educational elements.
- Learning orientation is defined as the degree to which the value of learning is stressed for the long-term benefits of the overall learning environment.
- Memory orientation is defined as the degree to which communication and distribution of knowledge is stressed in the learning environment (i.e., accessibility to knowledge).

The objective of education-related organizational learning should be to achieve superior learning in international marketing, subsequently providing a competitive advantage for students in their major (i.e., in this case the students represented marketing and international business majors). An integrated marketing course work designed around the four organizational learning orientations will lead to student's achieving a competitive advantage vis-a-vis their counterparts in the marketplace. As such, the function of the organizational learning framework in structuring marketing education means that education-related people (i.e., administrators, faculty, and students) put aside their old ways of thinking about details (learning orientation), adopt a broader perspective of how the marketplace really works in relation to the education offered (systems orientation), learn to be open with each other (memory orientation), and work together to form and implement a marketing education strategy upon which everyone can agree (team orientation).

The unique experiences of a non-urban state university are the basis for the study by Alma Mintu-Wimsatt, "Learning from Students' Perceptions of International Business." Her paper explores business students' perceptions to better understand undergraduates' views on international business (IB) as well as serve as a springboard for recommendations on how to improve IB education in the university. The "bottom-up" approach utilized here is atypical in academia since IB programs are often initiated by various representatives from functional departments and/or the administration.

In general, the students surveyed were unimpressed by the quality of their education, particularly on preparing them for interactions with foreign individuals. This piece of information is critical since the business students' exposure to IB is primarily received from their learning experiences in the classroom setting. However, many of the business students in the study university do not anticipate that IB will significantly affect their future careers. Findings suggest that upper division business students placed higher level of importance on IB.

The findings suggest that the business college of the study university and its faculty members face a major challenge. While several studies have shown that corporate America values IB education, many of the students in this university think otherwise. Hence, core classes have been changed to include a larger IB presence and create some awareness on the importance of IB in today's global business arena. Providing students with global exposure through guest speakers, corporate partnerships, etc. can help enhance the seemingly lukewarm attitudes toward IB.

The article by Kenneth R. Gray, "Information System Development in a Global Environment," informs the readers that a globally-designed information system integrated with contemporary business methodology offers organizations an opportunity to increase control and enhance coordination while opening access to new global markets and businesses. International organizations are forced to adopt global information technologies capable of sharing scarce resources across many borders. Global information systems facilitate international communication between a headquarters and its foreign subsidiaries. They, in theory, have no cultural or national boundaries. An ideal global information system contributes to achieving a firm's global business strategy by using information technology platforms to store, transmit, and manipulate data across cultural environments. In this article the basic components of an information system in a multinational context are reviewed.

An effective global information system is a continually-evolving system. Senior managers and information systems developers are advised to define the general parameters of a comprehensive, ideal system, and then to focus on initial information priorities. The initial planning stages must be guided by a clear vision of the future of the organization in global context with involvement of top level management, and senior managers in information systems. Information systems managers must change from their position of clinging to an orientation model that is largely national, and top down, i.e., from headquarters out to the subsidiaries. Information systems development must be conceptualized as global, reflective of the global operations, to achieve strategic advantage. To survive in a global market and achieve timely information systems development, systems must be developed, for the most part, locally.

International students are becoming an increasingly important part in American higher education, particularly to libraries that seek to enhance the educational opportunities and experience of all students. The paper by Harmon and Wales, "International and Domestic Students' Perception of Library Personnel and Resources: Explaining and Predicting the Differences," uses a large sample of international students and domestic students to discuss similarities and differences among the two groups. The authors offer several implications for the design and implementation of successful strategies by library administrators and teachers of international business. Administrators are advised to make the library accessible and suitable for studying with the focus on international students' needs. This group is more likely to use the library as a place to study than are domestic students (59% versus 32%). Furthermore, the typical international student uses the library for class assignments on a weekly basis more frequently than does the domestic student. International students believe that noise in the library is a problem that library personnel do not adequately address. Clearly the international student attaches more importance to a studying environment than does the domestic student, and believes the responsibility for maintaining that environment falls to the library personnel. Although a "library police" may not be an attractive opinion, administrators need to be aware of the international student's sentiment. By addressing this need, administrators may derive additional benefit because the international student frequently uses the library as a place to meet friends. A pleasant library experience, i.e., social episode, may amplify the positive feeling toward the library.

Library personnel must respond to international students in a helpful and polite manner so that the international student is encouraged to seek help. Both groups reported that the more frequently they sought help the more frequently they perceived the library personnel to be helpful and polite. However, when the international student is a frequent library user, he or she does not find the library personnel helpful and polite. Administrators need to identify the frequent user and eliminate those conditions that generate a negative perception of library personnel, e.g., the elevated noise level.

Librarians need to direct more attention to the international students' use of the online catalog and print indices for journals. Both of these areas were a source of difficulty for international students and subsequently indicated less helpful and less polite personnel. The results indicated that domestic students were adequately informed about these resources, whereas international students seem to prefer more hands-on instruction. It is not surprising to note that international students used the Internet and e-mail access more than domestic students did.

In the aggregate, the perception of helpful and polite library personnel is enhanced when students from both groups use the library more frequently, and when the student seeks assistance with a problem. An efficacious library strategy, therefore, is one that encourages library use for educational purposes and for quasi-social reasons. The library visit that includes the need to seek assistance generally results in a positive attitude toward library personnel. The use of library tours for student groups may be perceived as perfunctory and not generate the equivalent level of helpfulness that results from one-on-one interaction for specific needs.

There is no doubt that innovation is alive and well in all facets of our teaching. We know that there is a great variety of creative approaches being tried by educators around the world. Our challenge now is only to locate educational innovations and bring to greater visibility newer and better ways of teaching international business. Perhaps the future will provide an opportunity for interested academicians and educational consultants to meet more formally and share their ideas in more detail. In the interim, the *Journal of Teaching in International Business* may be used as a medium for the dissemination of ideas and knowledge among interested and concerned individuals. The *Journal* would welcome your submission of manuscripts on these and related topics.

NOTE

1. Here we must acknowledge that our European counterparts are often more advanced in this area than we because of the nature of their business education. The European business schools also maintain better cooperation with companies and government institutions and there are regular contacts through very active cooperative education programs.

REFERENCES

Beck, J., Whiteley, A. & McFetridge, P. (1996). Internationalizing the business student. *Journal of Teaching in International Business*, 4: 91-105.

Kedia, B. & Cornwell, T. (1994). Mission based strategies for internationalizing U.S. business schools. *Journal of Teaching in International Business*, 3: 11-29.

Kwok, C., Arpan, J. & Folks, W. (1994). A global survey of international business education in the 1990's. *Journal of International Business Studies*, 3: 605-623.

Raelin, Joseph A. (1999). *Work Based Learning: The New Frontier in Management Development*. Reading, MA.: Addison-Wesley.

Townsend, A. M., DeMarie, S. & Hendrickson, A.R. (1998). Virtual teams: Technology and the Workplace of the future. *The Academy of Management Executive*, 12: 17-29.

Strategically Rethinking the Executive MBA International Business Experience

Roger Kashlak
Raymond Jones
John Cotner

SUMMARY. During the past few years, Executive MBA (EMBA) programs at U.S. universities have expanded both in number and in content. As part of this expansion, an international experience has become an integral part of many of these programs. In most instances, the international experience has been a course planned and organized from a convenience perspective. This research proposes a more rigorous strategic planning model for EMBA program directors to consider in order to enhance the learning experience for participating students. Using a case example, it delineates between international field studies and international residencies, develops propositions, and offers an application of the proposed planning model. *[Article copies available for a fee from The Haworth Document Delivery Service: 1-800-342-9678. E-mail address: getinfo@haworthpressinc.com <Website: http://www.haworthpressinc.com>]*

INTRODUCTION

As U.S. business schools have increasingly introduced international experiences into their respective Executive MBA (EMBA) programs during the

Roger Kashlak is Associate Professor, International Business (E-mail: kashlak@loyola.edu); Raymond Jones is Associate Professor, Strategy; and John Cotner is Associate Professor, Finance, all at The Sellinger School of Business and Management, Loyola College in Maryland, 4501 North Charles Street, Baltimore, MD 21210.

[Haworth co-indexing entry note]: "Strategically Rethinking the Executive MBA International Business Experience." Kashlak, Roger, Raymond Jones and John Cotner. Co-published simultaneously in *Journal of Teaching in International Business* (The International Business Press, an imprint of The Haworth Press, Inc.) Vol. 10, No. 3/4, 1999, pp. 11-28; and: *Teaching and Program Variations in International Business* (ed: Erdener Kaynak and John R. Schermerhorn, Jr.) The International Business Press, an imprint of The Haworth Press, Inc., 1999, pp. 11-28. Single or multiple copies of this article are available for a fee from The Haworth Document Delivery Service [1-800-342-9678, 9:00 a.m. - 5:00 p.m. (EST). E-mail address: getinfo@haworthpressinc.com].

1990's, a simple question has arisen. How should these overseas programs be planned and delivered? These overseas learning experiences serve both strategic and organizational purposes within the overall EMBA structure. Strategic to many program learning objectives, the international experience enables the EMBA students to better understand motives for and degrees of global participation by multinational enterprises (MNEs). Furthermore, similar to the expatriate manager's experiences, exposure to new cultures and businesses within those cultures broadens the students' perspectives especially regarding their critical thinking, problem-solving and decision making skills.

Organizationally, the international experience serves to increase the bond among the students attending a lock-step program. Anecdotal evidence has suggested that after the return home from a positive international experience, the students are a much more cohesive and supportive class, thereby enhancing the overall learning experience for the remainder of the program. Thus, a positive experience must be assured and subsequently, rigorous front-end planning for these field studies must occur. First is the issue regarding the country(ies) to visit. Second, the program directors must decide on the organizations that will be visited in the selected countries. Finally, the program directors must decide upon an appropriate balance between on-site industry visits and classroom-type lectures from industry executives as well as home and host country diplomats and academicians.

Surveys at the national EMBA conference in recent years have suggested that U.S. universities have approached their respective international experiences from the two extreme perspectives. For instance, a number of schools (private and public, large and small) favor a strict international field study where, once overseas, the students are exposed exclusively to industry visits. Before and after the international segment, programs vary in their degree of in-class rigor in the home country. A few schools that were surveyed favored an international residency approach. For instance, one large, public Southern program had in-class lectures in London every year. Another school varied its residency year after year between Europe and Asia. Both programs included industry executives, academics and government officials on their respective lecture agendae.

Regardless of the approach that different business schools took regarding the EMBA international experience, one common theme that emerged from the informal survey and anecdotal evidence collected was planning convenience. Year over year, program directors did not rigorously plan the overseas portion of these courses. Rather, they took a convenience approach that will be further discussed below. The primary purpose of our research is to offer a strategic perspective to help the front-end planning process for the EMBA international experience. Specifically, our paper proposes a strategic framework for EMBA program directors to consider when planning and implementing an overseas field study, a residency, or a combination of both for their international business (IB) students. Furthermore, a series of propositions offers both research direction and project planning guidelines. An actual study program completed under our direction is introduced to help illustrate the planning framework.

MOVING FROM A CONVENIENCE PERSPECTIVE TO A STRATEGIC PLAN

Without a clear rationale and planning model, planning for an international student experience may become haphazard or poorly focused. Interviewing 15 separate U.S. EMBA programs, we found that international experiences are frequently planned and delivered through a convenience focus. For instance, specific foreign countries are targeted for visits due to the ease of getting there as well as the cultural nearness of certain countries to the program's home country and subsequent ease of adaptation of the EMBA students. Also, it was reported that host country universities are an important determinant when deciding where to visit. The stronger the sponsoring U.S. university's linkages with a foreign university are, the more likely the EMBA program will consider the country of that university for an international field study. These linkages may include already established undergraduate or graduate exchange programs as well as existing U.S.-host country research collaborations or consulting contacts previously forged by specific business school professors. What was not considered by programs employing a convenience perspective was the current global significance of the countries where linkages had been historically established.

It also appears that organizations within the countries are targeted due to the convenience of existing contacts. Indeed, organizing a program from thousands of miles away requires an immense amount of time. Therefore, as our interviews with other program directors suggested, many business schools replicate a successful overseas experience, regardless of the changing global environment, for a few years rather than starting from the beginning each year.

To attain the optimal learning experience for EMBA students, though, a strategic perspective must replace this one of convenience. We propose the following strategic dimensions to be included when planning international experiences: (1) a macroenvironmental level regarding the countries to be visited, (2) a firm-specific level regarding both the industry function and the differing strategies employed by the organizations targeted for visit within the countries, and (3) the method of delivery such as in-class residency, industry visits or a combination of both. Figure 1 illustrates this proposed planning model.

CONTRASTING EMERGING AND DEVELOPED COUNTRIES

The first dimension we consider is the country-level focus. Wells (1998) recently suggested that a critical issue for managers of MNEs investing in developing countries is the assessment of unique risks. An international experience may offer the opportunity for the EMBA student to experience the contrasts between levels of risk associated with developed and emerging countries. Furthermore, meshing these contrasting experiences is logistically feasible, whether considering the East-West linkage in Europe, or an Asian program combining Japan or Singapore with emerging countries like China, Vietnam or Malaysia.

Contrasting business practices that emerging countries offer is a critical component for understanding global strategy. These practices are diverse partly because of government policies directed at satisfying various general objectives of economic reform. For instance, a significant goal is the generation of hard currency. Some Eastern European governments have suggested they would only approve joint venture proposals demonstrating a strong likelihood of earning sufficient hard currency. In many emerging Asian countries, governments promote outward-looking postures and support joint ventures with potential to become viable global competitors and subsequently export the majority of their output to secure incremental hard currency. During this time of economic crises in both Southeast Asia and Russia in particular, understanding hard currency generation and restrictions represents an important issue for EMBA students.

A second significant goal represents the longer-range orientation of attracting Western firms into emerging countries so that local partners can learn Western technology and managerial and marketing know-how (Nobel and Morgan, 1989). Regarding this goal, a preference is to attract foreign partners who could accelerate the modernization of an industrial base, particularly in areas such as machine building, computers, robotics and control systems. In Eastern Europe, the training of managers as well as ventures that would help provide increased variety and quality of consumer goods and services are critical elements in motivating a work force (Sherr, 1988).

The contrast of external environmental influences between developed and emerging country perspectives is critical to convey to IB students (Daniels and Radebaugh, 1996). These influences include: (1) the relative stability of the host country's foreign exchange, (2) the cultural distance between home and host countries, and (3) in-country political risk and associated host government restrictions on operations. Compared to the United States, there will

FIGURE 1. A Strategic Planning Model for the EMBA International Experience

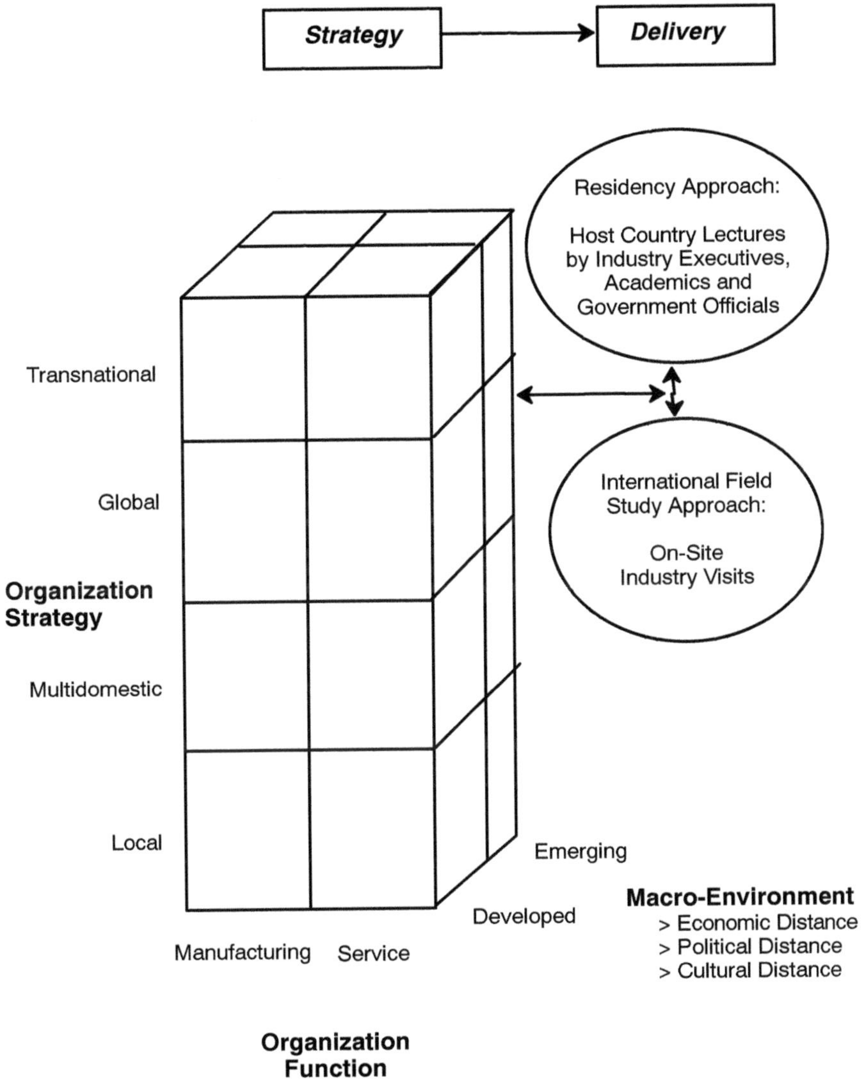

be greater political risk, economic instability and cultural distance in emerging countries than in developed countries. Further, as these factors fluctuate within countries, MNEs will adjust not only their respective strategies but also their respective control systems (Hamilton, Taylor and Kashlak, 1996). Therefore, a first-hand observation of how these factors contrast in developed versus emerging countries will give the EMBA students a more robust learning experience.

> Proposition 1: Inclusion of both developed and emerging countries into an international experience will increase the likelihood of goal attainment and success of the program.

Relative Inflation and Foreign Exchange Rate Fluctuations

A critical difference between a developed and an emerging country revolves around the relative economic stability of the countries and the subsequent risk to the multinational entity. As firms expand internationally, foreign exchange exposure increases leading to a subsequent increase in a firm's systematic risk (Reeb, Kwok and Baek, 1998). Furthermore, as foreign exchange movements have been linked directly to the inflation rate differential between two countries, absent monetary policy influences, the currency of the country with a higher inflation rate should proportionately decrease in value relative to the lower-inflation country's currency (Levi, 1990). Laurent and Lorange (1984) suggested that reliable financial control systems for MNEs must include the complicating factors of exchange rate fluctuations and relative inflation along with government imposed national exchange controls and taxation codes. The economic exposure to a firm is much greater in an inflationary, unstable environment more typical of emerging economies. Thus, the exposure to both emerging and developed country economies should enhance the student's knowledge of differing foreign exchange risk exposures as well as the strategies available to manage the various degrees of risk imposed.

> Proposition 1a: Inclusion of contrasting economic environments into an international experience will increase the likelihood of goal attainment and success of the program.

Cultural Distance Between the Home and Host Countries

Cultural distance and resultant cultural risk is another important element in international business theory and teaching. Similar to an MNE expanding overseas to countries most similar in culture and business culture environment to the home country (Linder, 1961), many U.S. EMBA programs use the United Kingdom as a first international experience. As an overseas destination increases in similarity to home, home country strategy formulation and implementation will tend to be extended to the host country. Thus, countries that are similar to the home country limit the learning of different management perspectives and decision-making processes for a visiting EMBA student.

As countries are increasingly dissimilar, management patterns as well as strategy formulation and adaptation will tend to be adapted to the host country norms. For instance, goal incongruence, a function of cultural differences of the partners (Wright, 1979), may be observed. Kogut and Singh (1988) found empirical support for the effect of national culture and associated decision-making and perceived risk on entry choice. Tse, Lee, Vertinsky and Wehrung (1988) found that specific cultural differences will affect managers' decisions. Bangert and Pirzada (1992) suggested that national culture influences the different phases of negotiations, while Kashlak, Chandran and DiBenedetto (1998) linked cultural distance to degree of partner reciprocity.

Therefore, organizing an IB field study in more than one country provides an important learning experience. Studying in both emerging and developed countries will provide the EMBA student with a more robust perspective when relating culture and cultural risk to his/her home country.

> Proposition 1b: Inclusion of contrasting cultural environments into an international experience will increase the likelihood of goal attainment and success of the program.

Host-Country Political Risk

The EMBA student must also understand that the political environment of a host country is a critical dimension in distinguishing among respective opportunities in foreign markets (Doz, 1986). The political environment may be related to international business through the concept of political risk. Greater exposure to political risk in developing countries increases the organization's total risk (Reeb, Kwok and Baek, 1998). Host-government risk in this context includes not only sensational events (such as expropriation) but also subtleties hidden within a complex operating environment. These subtleties include restrictions on profit repatriation, price controls, requirements for technology transfer and likelihood of work stoppages. Furthermore, political risk may arise for the MNE from interactions between host government and the MNE, among home government, host government and the MNE, and among third country governments, host government and the MNE (Simon, 1984).

The straining of these linkages leads to host government restrictions that limit an MNE's strategic options within the country. For example, without restrictions, a local venture can use tactics that include dynamic pricing, working capital management, strategic stockpiling and flexible sourcing to combat the inflationary effects on its operations (Laurent and Lorange, 1984). These restrictions prevent local managers from using a full arsenal of strategies and thus reduce a unit's operating efficiency and profitability.

Political risk and subsequent government-imposed restrictions on an MNE arise in emerging countries moreso than in developed ones (Juhl, 1978; Fatehi, 1994). Therefore, consistent with our arguments regarding risk arising from economic instability and cultural distance, we believe that an international experience will provide a greater learning tool if EMBA students are able to contrast the ramifications of the political situation in diverse countries.

> Proposition 1c: Inclusion of contrasting political environments into an international experience will increase the likelihood of goal attainment and success of the program.

CONTRASTING ORGANIZATIONAL STRATEGIES AND FUNCTIONS

Assuming the strategic and educational importance of a country focus that includes visiting both developed and emerging countries, the second order of planning EMBA international experiences must be on the companies to be visited within the countries. We consider two firm-level dimensions. The first dimension involves the general industries and functions of the organizations. The second is the specific strategies being pursued by the organizations within their respective industry boundaries.

The Organization's Function

There is a significant difference between goods and services. A good is an object, a device or simply a thing. In contrast, a service is a deed, a performance or an effort. Kotler and Armstrong (1989) elaborate that services are any activity or benefit that one party can offer to another that is essentially intangible and does not result in the ownership of anything. These authors, along with Czinkota and Ronkainen (1990), suggest a need for a major differentiation between goods and services due to the added service dimensions of intangibility, perishability and simultaneity of production and consumption.

Williamson's (1980) conceptualization that distinguishes between firm-specific and non-firm-specific human assets helps to delineate between goods and services. At one extreme of his framework are complementary services that directly relate to a primary manufactured product. In a middle range are services offered within both manufacturing firms and service companies that may be either non-firm specific (that is, able to be substituted by the external market) or firm specific (that is, those services unable to be substituted). At the other extreme of the framework is the externally-marketed output of various service industry companies. An optimal EMBA planning model should allow IB field study planners to more specifically target manufacturing and service organizations for visit consideration.

> Proposition 2: Inclusion of both manufacturing and service organizations into an international experience will increase the likelihood of goal attainment and success of the program.

The Organization's Strategy

Global integration pressures and local responsiveness pressures will affect competition in industries crossing national boundaries (Prahalad and Doz, 1987). In some industries, the former dominates, so that a firm's position in one competitive market is significantly affected by its competitive position in other markets (Hout, Porter and Rudden, 1982). These firms follow a global strategy, deriving the cost benefits of scale or scope economies. Therefore, because of the strategic need to maximize the collective organization, an MNE will have a longer-term strategic orientation and thus not depend upon immediate tangible profits.

However, not all industries that compete internationally exhibit the market interdependencies fitting the global profile. Doz and Prahalad (1984) suggested that certain factors will contribute to an industry's need to be more responsive to local environments, thus foregoing an attempt at maximizing the global organization. For example, product or service requirements may substantially differ from one geographical region to another, making standardization impossible. Furthermore, the benefits from scale or scope economies derived from the sharing of costs across markets may be constrained by governments imposing protectionist policies limiting international trade opportunities. Roth and Morrison (1990) suggested that these local responsiveness pressures are industry forces necessitating local context-sensitive strategic decisions. The resulting multidomestic strategy is an approach that attacks each market individually rather than attempting to gain cost advantages from a global integration effort.

Increasingly during the 1990's, new technologies, the emergence of unexpected competition and the redefinition of industry boundaries have confronted firms in industries undergoing extreme turbulence (Hamel and Prahalad, 1994; 1996). Subsequently, competitors within these industries are developing totally new rules of strategy and combining the global and multidomestic approaches. The resulting transnational strategy is a response when the competitive environment calls for efficiency and local responsiveness. Industries such as telecommunications service and pharmaceutical manufacturing are examples of industries where firms must be transnational to compete globally. Both industries have host-country regulatory agendae and cultural differences to consider. Yet, because of increasing competition, a customer sophistication mitigating differentiation advantages and worldwide industry consolidation, firms in both industries must also develop cost-based competencies.

Finally, to complete the international firm-level strategy learning experience for EMBA students, the organizers must also consider local firms pursuing either an export/import strategy or the host-country market alone, or a combination of the two. Indigenous industries such as cement manufacturing and publishing services are often affected by larger MNEs either by direct competition or through supply or distribution agreements.

> Proposition 3: Inclusion of firms pursuing various strategies into an international experience will increase the likelihood of goal attainment and success of the program.

CONTRASTING PROGRAM DELIVERY METHODS

To complement a rigorous front-end strategic planning perspective, alternative delivery methods must be investigated for the international experience. As stated earlier in this paper, two specific methods have been prevalent: (1) the international field study approach consisting primarily of host country industry visits, and (2) the international residency approach consisting primarily of in-class lectures in the host country. Anecdotal evidence suggests that the former approach has many positive aspects including visual and hands-on experiences associated with the visits. For instance, when visiting factories in countries such as the Czech Republic and China, our students received an appreciation for many facets of business that were completely different from the United States such as supervisory techniques, product movement, and adherence, or lack thereof, to safety standards. Still, unless these visits were combined with a detailed lecture by the organization's top management, the higher-level global strategy lessons went undiscovered.

A pure international residency also has many positive aspects. Logistically, more "visits" may be arranged from more diverse organizations. Thus, more comparative knowledge may be gained by the EMBA students. Furthermore, the lectures will be more policy and strategically oriented, thereby giving the students a higher-level learning experience–one that fits with the intent of the entire EMBA curriculum. Still, without the on-site industry visits, it may be argued that the experience is not truly international at all. The classroom could, in fact, be in the home country.

To gain the greatest amount of benefit for the students, a balance between both approaches must be planned. Historically, we have tried to arrange an industry visit around an executive's schedule in order to gain the important strategic insights of the organization. Also, we include a pure residency, or in-class portion during the experience. Because industry executives are usually at the visit site, the in-class lectures are primarily based around gaining knowledge of the host-country environment. Thus, to complement the various lessons learned from the industry visits/executive lectures, an international experience may also incorporate macro-environmental overviews from host country universities and government agencies. These lecturers from host country professors, embassy staff and media personnel are important complements to strategically planning an appropriate mix of countries, industries, companies and strategic postures.

> Proposition 4: Inclusion of in-class lectures and on-site industry visits combined with strategic overviews by organization executives in an international experience will increase the likelihood of goal attainment and success of the program.

A CASE APPLICATION OF THE STRATEGIC PLANNING MATRIX

The international business experience is a stand-alone course in the EMBA program. Even though the 10-day overseas experience is the primary activity of the course, there are front-end and back-end activities as well. The overriding goal of the course is to increase student awareness of global issues, environments and strategies. The course immediately follows, while building upon and applying the knowledge gained in a semester-long International Business course. Specific to our international business experience, Table 1 presents a timeline and capsule of the activities that the faculty members and students undertake regarding the planning and implementation of the course.

The planning occurs at the beginning of the academic year, when dates and countries are "locked-in." Subsequently, using the model that has been developed and discussed throughout this paper, a mix of industry visits and classroom lectures are arranged. As these specifics are investigated, some EMBA become involved if their organizations have subsidiaries, joint ventures or other activities in the countries that are planned for visit. If any of their firms fit within the overall framework of the model, we try to include

TABLE 1. A Schedule of Activities for the EMBA International Business Experience

Date	***Activity(ies)***
September	Introduce the "International Business Experience" concept to the participating class of EMBA students. Convey the scheduled dates during the following May of the 10-day overseas portion of the international experience to the students.
September-November	Based on (a) current trends in international business and macroeconomic/political indicators, (b) cultural distance, and (c) travel costs and logistics, decide upon the countries that will be visited during the following May (China, Hong Kong and Vietnam).
November-February	Based on the model illustrated in Figure 1, arrange industry contacts and lectures that will give the students exposure to a variety of industries, firm-level strategies and government initiatives. Involve students whose firms have subsidiaries, joint ventures or other business linkages in the countries of visit to include their organizations if those entities fit in the model.
March	Present the finalized international experience course to the students including: (a) the schedule of industry visits and lectures while overseas, (b) the front-end assignment for each student-team, (c) the structure of the in-class lectures and assignment presentations before the overseas portion, and (d) the parameters for the individual assignment due after the return from overseas.
May	Approximately eight hours of in-class time for academic lectures and presentations and discussions of the team assignments.
May	10-day international business experience.
June	Final individual assignments due.

them on the schedule. We believe that this better internalizes the experience for the entire class.

Once the overseas itinerary is set, teams of students are assigned specific research projects. These projects focus on either an aspect of the countries to be visited (for example, a comparative analysis of the political systems of China, Hong Kong or Vietnam) or an analysis of one of the industries that will be visited (for example, an overview of Global Shipping). These research projects are presented as part of a structured class before we depart from the United States.

Regarding the specific organizations with whom our group interacted, Figure 2 integrates the developed/emerging country-level dimension with the dual firm-level perspectives of organization function and organization strategy. It illustrates a 10-day EMBA international experience recently conducted in Asia. The program visited three countries, including Hong Kong, China and Vietnam. The industry visits were complemented by various university and governmental lectures, indicated within the figure, as well as by cultural experiences.

As illustrated in Figure 2, the participants in this international field study were able to visit countries in various stages of development. Within those countries, industry visits included a mix of service and manufacturing firms as well as organizations pursuing transnational, global, multidomestic and local strategies. The EMBA students participating in the field study-residency combination were able to clearly contrast the strategic dimensions outlined in this paper. For instance, Black & Decker's Power Tools division exhibited moves toward low-cost regional production facilities. Still, through a strategic overview in Hong Kong that preceded our plant visit in China, Black & Decker executives explained the corporate thrust to more efficiently coordinate their global activities especially between Asia and Europe. Similarly, from a service perspective, SeaLand illustrated an efficient worldwide networked configuration indicative of a global strategy. Their mission was to drive shipping costs down and improve time of delivery worldwide. Thus, its Hong Kong location was not viewed as standing alone but as an important piece of its global network.

Cigna Insurance was concentrating on better serving the specific Hong Kong market while studying China's ultimate potential from its Hong Kong subsidiary. Other markets in Asia were served by host-country based offices and remained independent from the Hong Kong location. Cigna's multidomestic approach was indicative of the industry where host government regulations and cultural habits regarding insurance varied greatly from country to country. In contrast, global telecom services epitomized a transnational industry where both global cost and local responsiveness pressures existed simultaneously. As an example, AT&T was examining potential joint ven-

FIGURE 2. An Application of the Strategic Planning Model for the EMBA International Experience

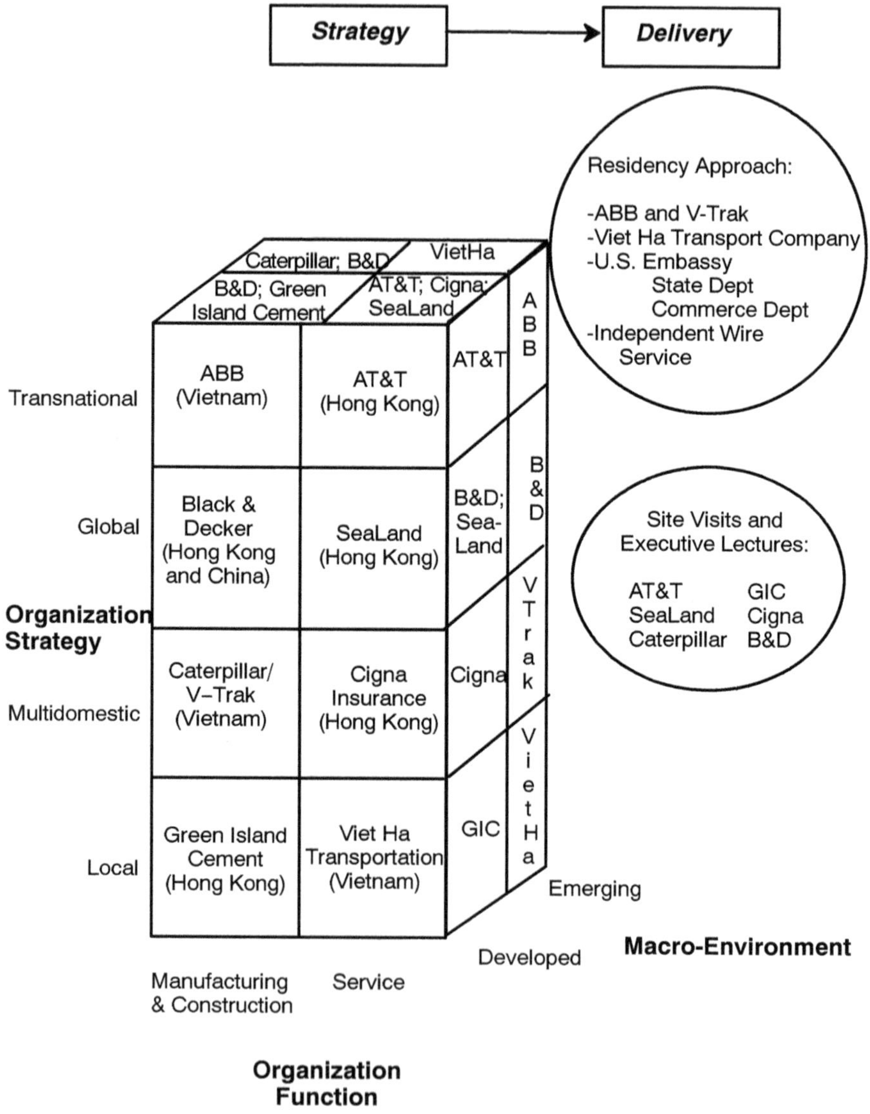

tures within the region to be positioned for local markets as they were becoming more deregulated while providing a more efficient global network for its multinational customer base.

An interesting contrast between two construction/infrastructure firms was seen in Viet Nam. ABB was efficiently linking resources and leveraging its skills on a global basis. Caterpillar was represented by a local subsidiary, V-Trak, which was exclusively concentrating on the Vietnamese market. Finally, the two local ventures, VietHA in Vietnam and Green Island Cement in Hong Kong, proved to be valuable learning experiences in understanding the respective host country organization structures, decision-making processes, competitive constraints and ultimate plans of expansion.

Using eight industry visits identified in Figure 2, each portion of the three-dimensional matrix is able to be completely filled. The Organization Strategy/Organization Function matrix is clearly identified with the companies that were visited. Beyond that, the 2×4 Organization Strategy/Macro-Environment matrix and the 2×2 Macro-Environment/Organization Function matrix are both optimized based on the combination of companies and countries visited. Based on program evaluation surveys distributed after we returned home, we found that the EMBA students, who were generally pleased with the entire experience, were especially pleased with certain industry visits. The combination of an organization's executives talking about their firm's global strategies with a subsequent in-depth location/plant visit seemed to be most appreciated by the students. Thus, Black & Decker and SeaLand, which both combined intense strategic and hands-on learning, were evaluated as the best experiences.

A CALL FOR INCREASED RESEARCH

In this paper, we have presented a conceptual framework for EMBA international experiences and an actual program showing its operationalization. The three-dimensional model considers contrasts in country-level factors as well as in firm-level functions and strategies. We believe this strategic planning perspective is preferable to the convenience approach taken by many EMBA programs for IB field studies.

Still, our proposed model is not all-inclusive of the strategic issues that executive programs may wish to consider. For instance, a program may consider a balance between regulated and deregulated industries to visit and study. Also, the issue of government ownership as compared to private ownership of firms may be integrated into the planning framework. The nationality of the firm may be considered as well. There will be distinct strategic lessons learned from a local firm as compared to foreign investors or international joint ventures combining assets from both local and foreign firms.

This article represents an initial effort to understand the importance of properly planning and structuring international experiences for EMBA programs. Rather than a model of convenience, we propose increased front-end planning in order to give the EMBA students an academically robust experience. The propositions presented here can be considered as design guidelines that seek high levels of goal attainment for the international experience and program success. Furthermore, they can hopefully stimulate a stream of research to develop a rigorous approach to planning and measuring performance outcomes for international experiences in the EMBA curriculum. For instance, does the inclusion of various countries and various firm-level strategies and functions, as suggested in this paper, create a more successful program in the eyes of the customer–the EMBA student? A survey instrument as well as student-based program output measures may be developed to test the propositions advanced in this article. Also, quantifiable program goals may be set at the front-end of a program and evaluated by the sponsoring business school after the study tour.

The efficacy of various delivery methods must also be studied. We propose a balance between the residency approach and the field study approach. Still, at a higher level of front-end coordination and ongoing student learning is an actual hands-on approach identified by Sherman, Chappell and Kashlak (1998). Those authors argue for the inclusion of actual real-life business problems that the students will participate in with an overseas organization. These team-oriented projects are proposed to even better solidify the learning derived from the international experience.

In conclusion, the international experience must be viewed as an integral part of the total EMBA program and not just an overseas vacation interrupted briefly for conveniently arranged industry visits. More research is needed to quantify and test the propositions advanced here, develop alternative delivery methods, and subsequently link the experience to the overall competitiveness of the EMBA program.

REFERENCES

Bangert, D. & Pirzada, K. (1992). Culture and Negotiation. *The International Executive*, January/February, 43-64.

Czinkota, M. & Ronkainen, I. (1980). *International Marketing*, Chicago: Dryden Press.

Daniels, J. & Radebaugh, D. (1996). *International Business: Strategies and Environments* (7th edition), New York: Addison-Wesley.

Doz, Y. (1986). Government Policies and Global Industries. In M. E. Porter (ED.) *Competition in Global Industries* (pp. 225-266). Boston: Harvard Business School Press.

Doz, Y. & Prahalad, C.K. (1984). Patterns of Strategic Control within Multinational Corporations. *Journal of International Business Studies*, 15(4), 55-72.

Fatehi, K. (1994). Capital Flight from Latin America as a Barometer of Political Instability. *Journal of Business Research*, 30, 187-195.

Hamel, G. & Prahalad, C.K. (1985). Do You Really Have a Global Strategy? *Harvard Business Review*, July/August, 139-148.

Hamel, G. & Prahalad, C.K. (1994). *Competing for the Future*, Boston: HBS Press.

Hamel, G. & Prahalad, C.K. (1996). Competing in the new economy: managing out of bounds. *Strategic Management Journal*, 17, 237-242.

Hamilton, R., Taylor, V. & Kashlak, R. (1996). Designing a Control System for a Multinational Subsidiary. *Long Range Planning*, 29(6), 857-868.

Hout, T., Porter, M. & Rudden, E. (1982). How Global Companies Win Out. *Harvard Business Review*, September/October 1982, 98-108.

Juhl, P. (1978). Investment Climate Indications: Are They Useful Devices to Foreign Investors? *Management International Review*, 18(2), 45-50.

Kashlak, R., Chandran, R. & DiBenedetto, A. (1998). Reciprocity in International Business: A Study of Telecommunications Alliances and Contracts. *Journal of International Business Studies*, 29(2), 281-304.

Kogut, B. & Singh, H. (1988). The Effect of National Culture on the Choice of Entry Mode. *Journal of International Business Studies*, 19(2), 411-432.

Kotler, P. & Armstrong, G. (1989). *Marketing: An Introduction* (2nd edition). Englewood Cliffs, NJ: Prentice Hall.

Laurent, J. & Lorange, P. (1984). The International Control Conundrum: The Case of Hyperinflationary Subsidiaries. *Journal of International Business Studies*, Fall, 185-201.

Levi, M. (1990). *International Finance: The Markets and Financial Management of MNCs.* New York: McGraw-Hill.

Linder, S. (1961). *An Essay on Trade Transformation.* New York: Wiley.

Nobel, E. & Morgan, H. (1989). Perspectives on U.S.-Soviet Joint Ventures. *CPA Journal*, July, 30-35.

Prahalad, C. & Doz, Y. (1987). *The Multinational Mission: Balancing Local Demands and Global Vision.* New York: The Free Press.

Reeb, D., Kwok, C. & Baek, H. (1998). Systematic Risk of the Multinational Corporation. *Journal of International Business Studies*, 29(2), 263-279.

Roth, K. & Morrison, A. (1990). An Empirical Analysis of the Integration-Responsiveness Framework in Global Industries. *Journal of International Business Studies*, 21(4), 541-564.

Sherman, H., Chappell, D. & Kashlak, R. (1998). Teaching International Business: Competence vs. Awareness. *Proceedings of the Southern Management Association.* Annual Conference, New Orleans.

Sherr, A. (1988). Joint Ventures in the USSR: Soviet and Western Interests with Consideration for Negotiations. *Columbia Journal of World Business*, Summer, 25-40.

Simon, J. (1984). A Theoretical Perspective on Political Risk. *Journal of International Business Studies*, 15(1), 123-142.

Tse, D., Lee, K., Vertinsky, I. & Wehrung, D. (1988). Does Culture Matter? A Cross Cultural Study of Executives' Choice, Decisiveness and Risk Adjustment in International Marketing. *Journal of Marketing*, October, 81-95.

Wells, L. (1998). Multinationals and Developing Countries. *Journal of International Business Studies*, 29(1), 101-114.
Williamson, O. (1980). The Economics of Organizations: The Transaction Costs Approach. *American Journal of Sociology*, 87, 548-577.
Wright, R. (1979). Joint Venture Problems in Japan. *Columbia Journal of World Business*, Spring, 25-31.

Pursuing Global Competence in Undergraduate Business Education: Use of an International Consulting Experience

Hugh D. Sherman

SUMMARY. Most approaches used by business schools to teach international business assist students in developing an awareness of global business issues. They help students to begin to recognize the international implications of their decisions. However, it is also important to actively move students towards "global competence." If students are going to be effective in an international economy they need to develop skills to be able to learn how to understand and operate effectively in other cultures. The program described here utilizes a project-based action learning approach to assist undergraduate students to learn "global competence." *[Article copies available for a fee from The Haworth Document Delivery Service: 1-800-342-9678. E-mail address: getinfo@haworthpressinc.com <Website: http://www.haworthpressinc.com>]*

INTRODUCTION

As a result of the worldwide trend towards government deregulation, and the ongoing revolution in information technology and communication, na-

---

Hugh D. Sherman is Assistant Professor of Strategy/Policy at the College of Business, Ohio University, Athens, OH 45701 (E-mail: shermanh@ohiou.edu).

[Haworth co-indexing entry note]: "Pursuing Global Competence in Undergraduate Business Education: Use of an International Consulting Experience." Sherman, Hugh D. Co-published simultaneously in *Journal of Teaching in International Business* (The International Business Press, an imprint of The Haworth Press, Inc.) Vol. 10, No. 3/4, 1999, pp. 29-41; and: *Teaching and Program Variations in International Business* (ed: Erdener Kaynak and John R. Schermerhorn, Jr.) The International Business Press, an imprint of The Haworth Press, Inc., 1999, pp. 29-41. Single or multiple copies of this article are available for a fee from The Haworth Document Delivery Service [1-800-342-9678, 9:00 a.m. - 5:00 p.m. (EST). E-mail address: getinfo@haworthpressinc.com].

tions are becoming increasingly integrated into the global economy. In the United States, for example, not only are more and more domestic firms involved in international business activities and/or have a culturally diverse workforce, but an increasing number of foreign firms are recruiting nationals from other countries (Larson and Benson, 1994).

Given the importance of international activities to the business community, business practitioners have criticized colleges and universities for not giving enough attention to the international dimensions of business. Critiques of business education, such as from Porter and McKibben (1988), have stimulated a great deal of discussion among academics as to what is the best approach to 'teach' the knowledge and skills that are required for our students to be able to be successful international managers (see for example Nehrt, 1992).

Beck, Whiteley, and McFetridge (1996) argue that undergraduate educators should stop focusing on internationalizing the curriculum and instead focus on developing strategies to internationalize the student. They suggest, and we agree, that it is not enough to internationalize the business curriculum by just offering some international material in core functional business courses. While this helps to provide students with an awareness of international issues, it does not build their competence for operating in international environments and effectively relating to people of different cultures.

The purpose of this paper is to describe a project-based, action learning approach to internationalizing the undergraduate experience for business students. We propose that this approach is an effective method that can enrich and extend the learning value of overseas study programs.

BACKGROUND

Kedia and Cornwell (1994) recommend that business schools that want to internationalize their curriculum begin by developing a mission statement. They offer three different levels of commitment that schools can adopt in seeking to internationalize their curricula: (1) global awareness, (2) global understanding and (3) global competence.

The first level of commitment is global awareness. It is pursued by integrating international topics into existing courses. This is the easiest and least costly approach. It utilizes existing faculty and helps students to begin to develop a world-view that recognizes the international implications of their decisions. In a survey of business schools, Kwok, Arpan and Folks (1994) found that 74% of the respondents use this approach to internationalize their curriculum. Its success hinges largely upon experienced faculty or available training for faculty. Due to lack of interest, time or expertise, the tendency may be for faculty to just omit international material from their courses. Up to 64% of schools in one study report having no training available for those who are interested enough to participate in this approach to internationalization, and only 14% had advanced education available (Kwok, Arpan and Folks, 1994).

Global understanding is the second level of commitment. Here, students not only develop a world-view but are able to begin to make decisions that incorporate knowledge and understanding of global markets. Kedia and Cornwell (1994) contend that schools that adopt this as their international mission will create a major or concentration in international business by adding courses in international business functional areas. Although schools operating at these first two levels of commitment represent improvements from past practices, we believe that schools should strive for higher levels of commitment. Add-on courses can help students obtain knowledge concerning the global economy, but they do little to help students develop the special personal characteristics and skills which are needed to effectively conduct international business (Beck, Whiteley and McFetridge, 1996).

Consistent with this expressed need for a higher-level international mission, Kedia and Cornwell (1994) contend that it is important that schools move towards the third level of global competence. To achieve this mission, the objective of the internationalization program is to help the student to be able to function effectively in an international business environment. This requires students to learn how to direct their own learning efforts to be able to discover what they need to know, how to obtain those answers and then to validate their answers using their actual experiences in the new culture. In essence they become active in managing their own understanding of other cultures.

To achieve true progress toward global competence students must be exposed to different cultures and experience real differences in things like problem solving, negotiations, and response to authority. This will help them to determine what types of leadership styles, organizational structures and reward systems are appropriate for different cultures (Kedia and Cornwell, 1994). They also learn to become sensitive to interpersonal cues to ascertain the behavioral rules and norms which effect the way business is conducted in a particular culture (Lane, 1992). These skills and abilities can only be learned through practical application or personal experience.

Challenges in Building Global Competence

The challenges of building global competence are complex and dynamic. In a series of conferences held by UNESCO (UNESCO, 1973), business and government practitioners reported a variety of skills necessary for managers to be effective overseas. These characteristics of a global manager include the following: ability to relate to new people, to bargain and negotiate in a cross-cultural setting, tolerance for ambiguous situations, adaptability and strength of personality to act forcefully but sensitively in unfamiliar contexts.

The prior skills and competencies are suggestive of international managers who develop three levels of cultural understanding (Serrie, 1992). The first is an understanding of themselves, they require this to overcome cultural shock, be personally adaptive and to tolerate ambiguous situations. Second, they must develop the skills necessary to manage cross-cultural differences at the interpersonal level. This requires them to develop negotiating and bargaining skills in a cross-cultural setting. They must also develop sensitivity to behave in an acceptable manner while still communicating their points of view. Third, at the organization level, the international manager must understand the host culture. This is necessary if one is to make correct managerial decisions regarding the organization's employees, market and community in which it operates.

When Kwok, and Arpan (1994) surveyed 381 U.S. business schools and 87 European schools, they found that European business programs gave their students much broader and deeper exposure to issues of international business than U.S. counterparts in virtually all respects. These schools were also found to place more emphasis on their students obtaining actual experience working in other countries. Historically, it seems that international business programs in U.S. inadequately dealt with cultural differences in business and management.

Past empirical research has also shown that many students retain limited cultural awareness even though they have learned cultural principles and concepts. For example, Morrill and Steffy (1980) found that students had acquired information concerning cultures but had not changed in their 'worldmindedness' attitude. That is, the students remained relatively limited in their openness and acceptance to different norms of behavior. Similarly, the United States Peace Corps has made use of university area studies programs to train volunteers for foreign service. But knowledge of the area alone has been found to be inadequate for altering attitudes and to prepare students to be able to develop extensive local community relationships (Harrison and Hopkins, 1967).

As alternatives to knowledge-based approaches, out-of-country experiences can be effective ways to deepen and broaden students' understanding about the complexities and realities of international business. These experiences take the forms of overseas internships, study abroad programs, and work abroad programs. Students participating in them have the opportunity to apply the theories they have mastered and learn more about particular issues concerning international business. They can improve their open-mindedness, develop broader horizons, and flexibility and tolerance for people from different cultures. However, few students participate in these activities. Unfortunately, one survey has shown that only 3% of all undergraduate students spent a semester abroad and only 2% took advantage of overseas internship opportunities (Kwok, Arpan and Folks, 1994).

Advantages of the Project-Based Learning Approach

In what may be called the traditional approach to teaching international business, the teacher transfers a body of knowledge to meet the needs of the student. The student plays a passive role with the movement of knowledge moving in only one direction. The critical assumption of this method is that once the knowledge has been acquired, the student will be able to apply this knowledge to any situation that they subsequently encounter. This assumption has questionable validity under many circumstances, but especially when applied to international business. As previously discussed, effective international management requires more than just knowledge. The international manager must develop sensitivity and skills to be able to diagnose a new situation and be able to understand the behavior and motivation of people from different cultures.

A promising direction in international business education uses a project or problem-based learning approach based on Dewey's (1929) classic plea for educators to develop independent learning in children. He argued that students should learn in response to and in interaction with real-life events. The principal idea is that learning is organized around problems which are related to the profession rather than around subjects which are centered on academic disciplines. This approach calls for students to solve real problems in small groups under the supervision of a tutor. The focus is on helping the students learn how to direct their own learning. The faculty is no longer the expert dispensing knowledge. Instead, the faculty takes on the primary role of the coach or tutor.

The general approach to problem based learning has been described by Schmidt (1993). A problem is assigned to the students. It is first discussed without reference to the literature. This helps the students to mobilize whatever information they may already have available among their team. The initial analysis of the problem stimulates the students to recall knowledge that they currently possess, activates their desire to learn and focuses their future learning efforts. Since the students view the problems as relevant, they become engaged in trying to solve the problem.

The faculty encourages students to develop questions concerning information they will need to obtain to solve the problem. These questions serve as learning goals to be pursued through self-directed learning. Students then review articles and books and collect primary data in order to build a more comprehensive understanding of the problem. The central tenet of this approach is that students learn how to structure their own learning as they proceed with the act of problem solving. What follows is a description of how we have tried to implement such a project-based, action learning approach at our university.

OHIO UNIVERSITY'S GLOBAL COMPETITIVENESS PROGRAM

Business students at Ohio University have the option of enrolling in a special international summer experience called the Global Competitiveness Program. One summer, for example, the students had the choice of either Hungary or Malaysia as the visitation sites; for another they could select either Spain, Hungary or South Africa. The program has four major components, which are summarized in Table 1, and takes place over approximately six weeks during the first of our two summer sessions.

TABLE 1. Components of the Global Competitiveness Program

1. International Business Training (14 days on Ohio University campus) a. Review key international business concepts i. Individual research on key learning issues ii. Class discussions of material b. Develop understanding of specific country issues to be able to conduct business i. In teams develop an oral and written country briefing research paper ii. Work with native graduate students in background briefings on culture and survival language classes
2. International Business Consulting Project (10 days in overseas country) i. Team building and dinner to meet client ii. Problem definition and research iii. Final report preparation iv. Presentation to company management v. Debrief and closing reception for all participants including company representatives
3. International Touring (10 days in overseas country) i. Visit businesses, ii. Historical and cultural sites
4. Personal Reflection Assignment (completed within four weeks after returning to U.S.) i. Identify and discuss what was learned about international consulting ii. Identify and discuss most meaningful personal experiences

Part 1: International Business Training

The first component of the program takes place on the Ohio campus. It requires that students learn about concepts concerning international business and to apply these concepts and do further specific research on the country they will visit. On the first day of the program, students are told that they will be required to develop a comprehensive briefing paper as to how a U.S. company conducts business in the country to be visited, e.g., Malaysia, Hungary or Spain. The paper includes a thorough economic, cultural and government profile for possible corporate entry into the country they have chosen.

The teaching approach taken uses the problem-based methodology. Once the students have the assignment then the faculty member helps the students structure the problem. Students are asked to identify and discuss what they know and then later, to identify what they need to know. They do some preliminary research and report this information to the class the next day. Over two days, and with the faculty member's guidance, two lists eventually emerge regarding the original assignment. The first list contains questions that require information specific to the target country. For example, students might identify that they need to understand what government policies exist that would affect a foreign firms' entry into that country. Or, they may recognize that they need to understand the demographics, education and income of the local market. The second list includes questions that require information and knowledge that is more general to international business and can be transferred to other country situations. For example, this listing might include: (1) for firms, what are the advantages and disadvantages of different entry modes, (2) how can different cultures be categorized and compared, and (3) what is the impact of trading blocks on company internationalization strategies.

In order to focus on individual accomplishments as well as teamwork, students must complete two assignments in part one. The first assignment is the group project, requiring an oral and written briefing paper on the country to be visited. This assignment is presented formally to the faculty one day prior to departure on the international trip. The second assignment requires students to individually submit three research papers on the learning issues that were identified above. Students submit this work on the Internet using Lotus's Domino Notes. Faculty grade the responses and ask questions that may require the student to do more work and further develop their understanding of the concept. In the "Domino" discussion groups, all students can read each other's entries, but each student must bring some original thought to their own response.

We allow students to resubmit their individual assignments until they receive an 'acceptable' rating from the faculty member. They have to obtain three acceptable ratings on three different issues to receive an 'A' for this part of their grade. This process of individual feedback using the Internet is extremely time consuming but allows the faculty member to develop and maintain a highly interactive ongoing tutoring relationship with the student. End of program course evaluations indicate many students believe that they have never worked so hard in their lives.

In part one, we do hold classes each day for two hours each morning and afternoon. This allows faculty to review and discuss key material. In addition, Ohio University graduate students native to the respective countries are employed to give the students cultural orientation sessions and some survival language training.

Part 2: Consulting Project

The second component of the Global Competitiveness Program puts Ohio University students into teams with host countries students to complete a consulting assignment in the target country. The consulting team usually consists of six members, with three from each university. The projects that students work on have been established and agreed to in advance by the faculty at Ohio University, the faculty of the local Hungarian or Malaysian University and the local company representative. In terms of the timetable, we try to start the formal project work on Sunday. This begins with team building exercises and includes the development of team action plans for the week-long consulting assignment. Sunday night the students meet with the company representatives at a formal dinner and arrangements are completed for the first visits on Monday morning.

Monday through Friday the students work with a local company to help solve a specific problem of that company. Faculty visit every company daily to make sure that the students are making sufficient progress. However, the faculty do not interfere unless there is an obvious problem or question. At the end of each work day, the faculty conduct a debriefing session with the students to review the day's events. Students write up a quick one page report identifying what they accomplished that day, any problems they ran into, and what they expect to accomplish on the next day. Students then share their experiences with the group. Faculty meet individually with groups if there are any special problems.

Computer labs are made available for all students for every day until 10:00 p.m. so they can work on their project reports. On Saturday, students meet with faculty to make preliminary presentations of what they will offer to their respective firms. Students then have two days to revise their reports and get any final information that they will need. On Tuesday, each consulting team presents their findings and recommendations to the firm's management at their respective company's offices. One faculty member is at every presentation. Students are graded on their oral and written presentations. In addition, the firm's management is asked to fill out a form to record its opinion on the team's performance.

Part two moves toward conclusion on Tuesday night with a final reception for all participants in the program, including company representatives. Two members of each team, one Ohio University student and one local student, share with the entire gathering their most significant learning experiences from the consulting project. Part two concludes Wednesday morning when faculty hold a debriefing session to discuss what the students learned.

Parts 3 and 4: International Touring and Personal Reflection Assignment

The third major component is probably the most enjoyable for the students and also quite necessary. For approximately ten days, the students travel around the host country, relaxing, and enjoying the culture. Upon returning home, students are required to complete the fourth major component. This is an individual assignment that requires them to formally reflect on their experiences. Students complete a 10 to 15 page paper discussing what they learned about cultures, consulting, team work, international business and more. They are encouraged to discuss their own personal experiences and what they believed they achieved.

PROGRAM EVALUATION

The 1998 summer program was evaluated by use of a survey, to both participating companies and students. Companies were asked to evaluate the quality and value of the students' consulting reports. They generally reported two benefits. First, they appreciated the diversity of opinion from American and local students. We were told that the American students tend to ask very direct questions that required the firm's management to reconsider assumptions that they have taken for granted. The firms also liked the information on how U.S. companies handle similar problems. Two criticisms were expressed. First, company representatives felt that student groups often took a narrow view of the problem that they are given. Students were encouraged to realize how individual functional problems impact the rest of the organization, but we were not always successful. Secondly, firms indicated that the students needed more than the eight days allowed for the actual on-site consulting.

The students were asked questions relating to what they learned and what they liked and disliked about the program. Table 2 lists some of the statements that students included in their assessment of the summer 1998 program. They rated the overall experience as a 4.7 on a 5.0 scale. The most

TABLE 2. Selected Student Assessments of Global Competitiveness Program

Key Learning Outcomes

"It's not as easy as I thought! There were some things that I felt were being done wrong that I automatically wanted to correct, but it is just because of my perspective and the way I am used to seeing things. You really have to be flexible. (That is hard for me)"

"Knowledge that I must be open and conscious of other people's cultural differences. I feel I have gained a better sense of communication skills."

"When consulting you have to consider personal relationships sometimes above the bottom line. You have to be flexible and patient and you need good communication skills in order to be able to explain what you are saying. The language barrier is more difficult to deal with than I thought."

"Open-mindedness–often times I totally disagreed with what the Hungarian members had to say, but I learned to look at things from their point of view."

"It is very important to think out of the box as well as go beyond your country. There is great value when you are being exposed to different company's culture, language and problem solving methods."

Overall Assessment of Program

"I have learned more in the last few weeks than I will probably learn in school taking tests. Being in the environment is so important, and this program should be requirement of every student in the future."

"If you have the chance to apply knowledge learned into an actual business atmosphere overseas, the learning value is priceless."

"It was wonderful to get some real experience in the field. At this point, I feel much more prepared for the kind of work I want to do. I love to travel, but it was good to get a preview of what international business is really like."

"I learned a lot about business . . . That I could not have learned any other way."

"I loved it! I think international business is essential . . . It taught me everything I know (so far)."

"I learned more in the ten days before we left and the days spent in Oveido (Spain) than the two years at OU (Ohio University)."

"There is no substitute for an experience like this. You can talk all you want, differences in culture and other issues related to both teamwork and general consulting skills, but you can never reach the level of understanding and practical understanding of these topics that this program achieves."

"It was more than an educational experience–it was a real experience. I learned more in one week prep and ten days in Pecs (Hungary) than I could have ever imagined and more than any classroom course. I not only gained a cultural understanding of Hungary, but made friendships that I feel will last a long time."

important skill the students reported learning is the ability to be more open and sensitive to cultural differences. They report gaining more understanding of the importance cultural differences on how business is conducted. One unexpected outcome that students reported was learning the importance of developing personal relationships in doing business abroad. Many students also reported that they found patience and the need to repeat ideas in order to reduce misunderstandings with their teammates. In addition, students talked about the importance of building trust and having respect for others, even though you do not understand their ideas.

The experience seems to stimulate students desire to study languages. With regards to what the students would do in the future to prepare for a business trip to a country that had not visited previously, many students reported the importance of learning the language. Out of the students who went to Spain, 16 of the 19 talked about the importance of language training and wished that they had taken further language classes before they went. Interestingly, over half of the students who went to Spain had taken Spanish language courses previously but wished that they could communicate more effectively. In the case of the students who went to Hungary only four out of 22 wished that they had taken Hungarian language classes. This is logical given that Hungarian is a much more difficult language to learn and not as widely spoken in the world.

DISCUSSION AND CONCLUSION

Mendenhall, Dunbar and Oddou (1987) suggest that there are different levels of cross-cultural training including: (1) an information giving approach; (2) an affective approach; and (3) an immersion approach. The information approach simply includes area and cultural briefings and "survival-level" language training. The affective approach includes cultural simulations and role-playing, case analyses, moderate language training and stress reduction training. Finally, the immersion approach involves field experiences, assessment centers and sensitivity and extensive language training. The more rigorous the preparatory training, the more overseas acculturation and subsequent productivity will be expected. Likewise, we can expect that the more the student participants in international business programs are truly immersed in foreign business environments, the more benefits they will gain.

What are the benefits of our type of integrated international program? Beyond increased knowledge of local cultures, customers, markets and governments, we believe students in the Global Competitive program develop critical managerial skills including: (1) greater tolerance of ambiguity because there is never the complete, rapid information that once can access in a home environment; (2) ability to gain multiple perspectives regarding decision-making; and (3) greater ability to work with and manage others. A very effective way to 'teach' global competence is to place students in a foreign environment where they must build effective interpersonal relationships with people from a different culture. Successful completion of the consulting project, furthermore, requires students to develop a working relationship with foreign teammates for translation, understanding of the behaviors of the firm and to access local resources.

Having experienced and committed faculty is critical to making this type of program successful. It requires much more time from students and faculty alike, than just conducting a scheduled class or conducting a visit to local firms. It requires an incredible amount of interaction by faculty with individual students and teams of students, and time spent on managing the learning situations and providing coaching. The program also requires much coordination, working with overseas partner universities, finding local firms willing to make arrangements and provide appropriate consulting projects for the students to work on.

An excellent working relationship with the local university is indispensable. The program works best if participating local students also get academic credit for participating in this program. This helps to motivate them to do the work that is required in the relatively short time frame. We also rely on the local universities relationship with local area firms to be able to identify possible consulting projects.

Overall the benefits for the students are substantial. They can be seen at the personal, interpersonal and organization level. At the personal level, students gain confidence that they can operate effectively in a unique foreign culture (not just as a member of a tour group) in which the student has had little or no previous familiarity. At the interpersonal level, students develop cultural sensitivity to physical as well as verbal cues. They become more adept at not making social blunders and exhibiting acceptable behavior. It is these learning skills that will make them much more successful in different cultures in the future. At the organizational level, students have been able to come up with decisions and recommendations appropriate for their client firms. They gain confidence in their abilities to deal with real business problems. They also grow in understanding how culture affects the implementation issues associated with their decisions.

Many of our students who have participated in this program tell us that, being part of the Global Competitiveness Program is one of the (if not the) most rewarding experience they have had in their undergraduate education. We believe that this program is a powerful 'teaching' method for developing global competencies and future international business managers.

REFERENCES

Beck, J., Whiteley, A. & McFetridge, P. (1996). Internationalizing the business student. *Journal of Teaching in International Business*, 4:91-105.

Harrison, R. & Hopkins, R. (1967). The design of cross-cultural training. *Journal of Applied Behavioral Science*, 3: 431-460.

Kedia, B. & Cornwell, T. (1994). Mission-based strategies for internationalizing U.S. business schools. *Journal of Teaching in International Business*, 5 (3):11-29.

Kwok, C., Arpan, J. & Folks, W. (1994). A global survey of international business education in the 1990's. *Journal of International Business Studies*, 3: 605-623.

Kwok, C. & Arpan, J. (1994). A comparison of international business education at U.S. and European Business schools in the 1990's. *Management International Review*, 34(4): 357-379.

Lane, H. (1992). Methods for learning involved in internationalizing management education: Experimenting with silent meeting, microcultures and microworlds. *Journal of Business Administration*, 21: 1-2.

Mendenhall, M., Dunbar, E. & Oddou, G. (1987). Expatriate Selection, training and career-pathing: a review and critique. *Human Resource Management*, 26(3): 331-345.

Morrill, W. & Steffy, D. (1980). The ethnography of collegiate teaching: bridging the student and academic cultures. *Journal of Thought*, 15: 49-75.

Porter, L. & McKibben, L. (1988). *Management Education and Development: The Drift into the 21st Century?* New York: McGraw-Hill.

Schmidt, H. (1993). Foundations of problem-based learning: some explanatory notes. *Medical Education*, 27: 422-432.

Serrie, H. (1994). Teaching cross-cultural management skills. *Journal of Teaching in International Business*, 3(3): 75-91.

United Nations Educational. (1973) *Scientific and Cultural Organization: A Report of four conferences*. ERIC Document: 119-284. Washington, D.C.

Introducing International Business Experience Through Virtual Teamwork

David S. Chappell
John R. Schermerhorn, Jr.

SUMMARY. The role of computer-mediated or virtual teamwork is increasing in modern organizations and the pressures of our increasingly global economy are unrelenting. Forces of technology and internationalization pose significant implications for business and management education. This paper describes the use of international virtual teamwork in the introductory management course at our university. The project is introduced along with the logistical and technological support required for their implementation. Student evaluations and faculty considerations are shared. The conclusion is offered that such projects can often be developed at minimum cost using available technologies and the international contacts of faculty. A call is made for giving more attention to international virtual teamwork opportunities in our business and management curricula. *[Article copies available for a fee from The Haworth Document Delivery Service: 1-800-342-9678. E-mail address: getinfo@haworthpressinc.com <Website: http://www.haworthpressinc.com>]*

Headline: Global data connections let companies swap projects office-to-office around the world, expanding the workday to 24 hours.

David S. Chappell is Assistant Professor of Management, College of Business, Ohio University, Athens, OH 45701 (E-mail: chappell@ohiou.edu). John R. Schermerhorn, Jr. is the O'Bleness Professor of Management, College of Business, Ohio University, (E-mail: schermer@ohiou.edu).

This is a revised version of a paper presented at the international meeting of the Western Academy of Management, "Bridging the Continents: Creating, Sharing and Enhancing an International Vision," Istanbul, Turkey, June 29-July 2, 1998.

[Haworth co-indexing entry note]: "Introducing International Business Experience Through Virtual Teamwork." Chappell, David S. and John R. Schermerhorn, Jr. Co-published simultaneously in *Journal of Teaching in International Business* (The International Business Press, an imprint of The Haworth Press, Inc.) Vol. 10, No. 3/4, 1999, pp. 43-59; and: *Teaching and Program Variations in International Business* (ed: Erdener Kaynak and John R. Schermerhorn, Jr.) The International Business Press, an imprint of The Haworth Press, Inc., 1999, pp. 43-59. Single or multiple copies of this article are available for a fee from The Haworth Document Delivery Service [1-800-342-9678, 9:00 a.m. - 5:00 p.m. (EST). E-mail address: getinfo@haworthpressinc.com].

> *Case in Point:* At Fluor Corporation, an international engineering and construction company in Irvine, California, more than 280 engineers and technicians cut three months out of a 14-month design period for a chemical plant. They did so by "following the sun" and using networking technologies to push digital plans from electrical-conduit designers in the Philippines to structural engineers in Houston and pipe-planners in Calgary, Alberta, then back to the Philippines.
>
> *Case in Point:* At Bechtel Corporation in San Francisco, one of Fluor's competitors, computerized plans for a $600 million expansion of Dubai airport in the United Arab Emirates are passed among more than 100 architects and engineers working in San Francisco, London, Dubai and New Delhi, India. "This project never sleeps," a company official says. (*The Wall Street Journal,* 1997)

These examples show the dramatic intertwining of two forces shaping the future of organizations in modern society–internationalization and globalization. Both pose significant challenges to corporate leaders and business educators alike. We live, work, teach and study in an age of information and a global economy. Peter Drucker describes this age as one where "the productivity of knowledge and knowledge workers" will become the decisive competitive factor (Drucker, 1997). Intellectual capital, the collective brainpower or shared knowledge of a workforce that can be used to create wealth for an organization, is fast becoming the new focus of corporate leadership (Stewart, 1997). Graduates of business and management curricula must be ready for careers in a competitive economy where General Electric CEO Jack Welch says: "The aim in a global business is to get the best ideas from everywhere" (Waters, 1997). They must be prepared to succeed as masters of technology and informed global citizens.

As educators, we are duty-bound to anticipate students' future challenges and provide current learning opportunities in which they can explore competencies relevant to the new workplace. This paper describes the use of international virtual teamwork to integrate global awareness and technological understanding in the introductory management course at our university. Two projects are examined along with the logistical support that was required for their implementation. Student evaluations are shared and the conclusion is offered that such projects can often be developed at minimum cost using available technologies and the international contacts of faculty. A call is made for more attention to opportunities for adding international virtual teamwork activities to our business curricula.

EDUCATION FOR A TECHNOLOGY-DRIVEN GLOBAL ECONOMY

Peter Drucker calls knowledge "the principle resource of a competitive society;" and also warns that "knowledge constantly makes itself obsolete" (Drucker, 1997). In this paradoxical environment, business and management educators face two imperatives that should be viewed as compatible, complimentary and synergistic: (1) how to internationalize the curriculum, and (2) how to integrate and best utilize technology in the learning context.

The Internationalization Imperative

While the need to internationalize business education remains undisputed, the degree to which the objective is realized varies significantly among academic institutions (Fleming, Shooshtari, and Wallwork, 1993). After reviewing a survey on the topic, Kwok, Arpan and Folks concluded that although progress has been made, "the majority of students leaving the formal business education systems had no or minimal knowledge of international business" (1994: 621). They suggest further that, on average, internationalization efforts fall short of providing businesses with personnel who can think and act in a global context. Although we are writing some four years later, our premise is that progress is being made but that much more remains to be accomplished.

The following four approaches to internationalization in business curricula are described by Kwok et al. (1994). (1) Faculty may include an international dimension into existing courses such as organizational behavior or market research. (2) They may offer a general or survey course in international business. (3) They may offer specialized international courses in one or more functional fields, such as international management or international finance. (4) They may require one or more international-oriented non-business courses to be taken as part of the business major, such as world geography or comparative economic systems. In addition, a fifth alternative should also be recognized. More schools are also making available to their students a variety of study abroad opportunities. They range from the full year or semester/quarter abroad residencies to summer schools, often in cooperation with partner institutions in different countries. These possible directions for internationalization are typically found in various combinations as schools work various agendas in efforts to improve their global perspectives.

A classification scheme offered by Kedia and Cornwell (1994) identifies three stages of curriculum internationalization–global awareness, global understanding, and global competency. Each stage represents an increased level of international sophistication and understanding among students and faculty. The first level of *global awareness* involves the integration of international topics into the existing curriculum. The objective here is to provide students with what Kedia and Cornwell call a "world view" in the areas of information collection and problem solving. Kwok et. al. (1994) reported that 74% of the respondents in their survey of business schools were using this approach as the main means of providing international education.

The second level of internationalization encourages students to achieve *global understanding*. Students move beyond the acquisition of worldviews to begin more confidently to incorporate global knowledge and understanding into their decision making. Information from a global perspective becomes part of the student's frame of reference as they engage learning activities across a wide variety of business areas and disciplines. International business specialists are included on faculties, and rewards for international research and teaching courses with strong international content are usually present.

The third and highest level of international education involves the level of *global competence*. The objective here is not only to gain a world view and willingness to embrace the global dimension in decision making, but also to develop actual international experience as a base for functioning in the international environment. Often times this requires the immersion of the student in a foreign culture in some form of study-abroad program. From a 1993 survey of schools listed in the AACSB Membership Directory, 67% of reporting institutions have study-abroad programs with about 38% of business schools having their own (Fleming et al., 1993).

In respect to the international imperative, the challenge for business education is stated as follows: " 'to expose students to [an] international dimension' in a way which can be meaningfully integrated into degree programmes which prepare them for the world of work" (Beck, Whiteley, and McFetridge, 1996: 92). Yet differences in missions, public versus private institutions, faculty experience, funding limitations, and other realities make it difficult for all academic institutions to fully incorporate an international perspective. Beck et al. argues that rather than concentrating on the internationalization of the *business curriculum,* course designers should consider ways to internationalize the *business student* (1996: 104; emphasis added). Simply put, there is still room for creativity and innovation in the commitment to internationalizing the learning environments for business students.

The Technology Imperative

Technology empowers people and it is certainly bringing many changes to higher education. A recent edition of *AACSB Newsline* (1998), for example, featured the growing impact of technology on education. It describes an executive MBA program at Duke's Fuqua School of Business that executives from 19 different countries recently through computer-mediated distance learning combined with several intensive residencies. The new Western Governors University is a technology-driven university without walls; similar strategies are evident in the distance learning programs of the University of Phoenix and the Instituto Technologio y de Estudios Superiores de Monterrey, Mexico. In the corporate sector, companies like AT&T are offering more and more of their training programs through the Internet. Just as technology empowers people, it is also empowering educators and students with a whole new range of alternative learning environments.

But technological innovations in education aren't limited to distance learning applications alone. An entire special issue of the *Journal of Teaching in International Business* (1996) was devoted to examining how technology can be used in international business education. Importantly, emerging technologies can help bring to many classrooms the very type of international experiences that are increasingly common in global corporations–virtual or computer mediated international teamwork. The business community finds itself on the frontier of virtual entities, including virtual jobs, virtual groups and even entire virtual companies (Oravec, 1996: 47).

The notion of virtual teamwork is of special interest to corporations whose commercial interests span national boundaries. Recent technological developments are unprecedented and have resulted in what has been called confidently the "death of distance" as an impediment to doing business internationally (*Economist,* 1997). A myriad of electronic communication options, particularly Computer-Mediated Communication Systems (CMCS), allow virtual team members to cope with the opportunities and challenges of task performance across great geographical distances. As the cost of computing and telecommunications continues to drop and as new software becomes available, international businesses have an ever-expanding array of options at their disposal to accomplish work that would otherwise involve extensive travel, costs and time delays. Virtual teams can now easily work across the limits of "space, time and organizational boundaries" using new communication technologies and supporting GroupWare programs (Lipnack and Stamps, 1997; Warkentin, Saveed and Hightower, 1997).

Organizational practitioners, however, must still be realistic and cautious in viewing the virtual team as a replacement for more traditional group work and interactions. Lipnack and Stamps point out that it can be "harder for virtual teams to be successful than for traditional face-to-face teams" (1997: xxi). In their examination of virtual teams, Warkentin, Sayeed and Hightower report that while face-to-face teams reported greater satisfaction with the group interaction process, the exchange of information was as effective in virtual teams (1997: 987). As research builds in this important new area of technology and organizational dynamics, however, it is likely that virtual teams will emerge with assets and liabilities that suggest them to be more appropriate for some situations than others (Galegher and Kraut, 1994; Orlikowski and Hofman, 1997). Their place in international business, however, seems assured even as we are still learning about them.

When virtual teams are tried in the typical campus setting, the exercise in virtual teamwork can become problematic as students are forced to use GroupWare technology and virtual processes in situations where they have no actual need. The first requirement is to match the technology with the objectives of the assignment. Increasingly complex tasks require a requisite level of support from increasingly rich CMCS options. That is, the learning environments for virtual teamwork may appear artificial to the students. What are needed are situations that utilize new technologies to work in situations similar to their workplace applications. In this context, there is great opportunity to blend the forces of globalization and technology to great advantage. Just as virtual teams are making inroads into the world of international business, so too can they make inroads into international business education.

INTERNATIONAL VIRTUAL TEAMWORK IN THE BUSINESS CLASSROOM

The situation just described offers the opportunity to create learning experiences that merge the interests of internationalization and technology utilization in the business classroom. Higher education for business and management is confronted with the challenge of providing a realistic introduction to working with virtual teams. It is also faced with the need to provide greater opportunities for students to climb the ladder of global awareness, understanding and competence. International virtual teamwork that joins students from different countries to work on common projects offers academic institutions a low-cost way to enrich both the technology and globalization aspects of the education experience.

Advances in information and telecommunication technologies now provide the ability to conduct "virtual" international business activities in a manner not imagined as few as five years ago. Options including E-mail, the Internet, web pages, chat rooms, GroupWare such as Lotus Domino and others, are now available and offer the educator a wide variety of instructional design alternatives. They also represent a potential virtual advantage through which institutions can benefit from lower-cost alternatives to globalization through study-abroad programs requiring expensive overseas travel. By employing new technologies to best advantage, a whole new range of options for integrating the global dimension into our business curricula can be found. And importantly, many more students can have the advantages of participating in a real international work experience. Rather than dealing with internationalization and technology utilization as separate and individual goals, they can and should be merged to create an integrative learning opportunity (Lewis, 1996).

International Virtual Team Project Description

During one spring and summer, the authors worked with colleagues in Thailand and Malaysia to design international virtual teamwork projects for implementation as an option in our introductory management course. These were personal contacts by the instructors. A small grant from Ohio University to internationalize the curriculum provided support for travel expenses when the authors visited Thailand from a university assignment in Malaysia to present the project proposal faculty at Bangkok University. This connection resulted in our working directly with a faculty member teaching an introductory management course for MBA students at Bangkok University. The Malaysia linkage was not with a formal course, but with individual graduates of an MBA program in Malaysia and in which the authors participated.

Our course, MGT300, is an introductory undergraduate course taught in large sections of 100+ students. During the Fall and Winter academic quarters, six teams operated–four teams with Ohio University students paired with counterparts at Bangkok University, and two others linking OU teams with Malaysian counterparts. The teams consisted of 4-6 members at both the OU and international sides. In all cases, the project requirements were the same (see next section). In order to focus on cross-cultural understanding in management, a series of self-assessment exercises were selected by the teams to be completed by participants and samples of students from their home cultures. The project requirements included developing both within-culture and across-culture data summaries and analyses of results. All communication was to be handled by the students themselves. In the Fall projects, the communication was handled both by E-mail and through Lotus Domino software; in Winter, all communication was handled through the Lotus Domino software.

In the case of the Bangkok University collaboration, students were required to submit the completed project for grading to instructors at both OU and BU. For the respective teams, the results were included as part of students' final grade computations. In Malaysia, the participants were not linked to a local course and were engaged in the project for personal interest. What follows is the actual description of the international virtual teamwork project as provided to the students.

International Virtual Teamwork Project

This project requires extra effort to participate in an *international virtual team*. The virtual team will be mediated by the Lotus Domino software located on the College of Business server. Special access to this software will be arranged by the instructor. Students from each university will form into 4-5 person teams. Each team will complete a "domestic" project (see Part A) and then participate in an "international" comparison project (see Part B) working with a team from the other university. A final report will be created by each pair of teams working together. The same final report will be submitted by each team in the pair to their respective instructors for grading.

Part A: "Domestic" Comparisons

1. At the end of each part of the textbook (Schermerhorn, 1999) there are sets of self-assessment instruments. Your first task is to reach agreement with your counterpart team at the other university on a set of 5 assessments which you will both work with. *The assessments should be chosen for their personal development and career relevance to team members.*
2. Working individually, each member of the two groups should complete each of the self-assessments according to textbook instructions.
3. Each member of each group should have the same set of assessments completed by five additional students who are not part of the same management class.
4. Results from #2 and #3 should be entered into an Excel spreadsheet and analyzed to provide descriptive statistics that compare (1) differences between team members and the additional students, as well as (2) differences among team members. These results should be summarized in well-chosen tabular and graphical forms.
5. Team members should discuss results described in #4 and identify insightful patterns and findings in the data. These patterns and findings should be interpreted in respect to the following question: "What do these results indicate about the management potential of Ohio University or Bangkok University undergraduate students?"
6. This discussion should be summarized in 1-2 page single-spaced memorandum addressed to the instructor.

Part B: "International" Activities

1. Teams from each university should share their results in Part A with their counterpart team at the other university. They should compare both the data in #4 and the interpretation in #5.
2. These comparisons should be summarized in an integrative spreadsheet analysis that summarizes all data collected by both teams and allows for the data to be examined both within each culture (Thai and American) and across cultures.

3. Members of the teams should discuss the patterns in the within-culture and across-culture comparisons and interpret them in respect to the following questions: (a) "What are the major similarities and differences between students from the two cultures?" (B) "How can these differences be explained?"
4. This discussion should be summarized in 1-2 page single-spaced memorandum addressed to instructors at each university.
5. A final *International Self-Assessment Portfolio* should be prepared and submitted to summarize and integrate results of the virtual teamwork. This portfolio should include:
   a. title page
   b. the memorandum written in #4
   c. copies of all spreadsheets and graphs developed in Part A and Part B
   d. copies of memorandums written for Part A
   e. a "signature" page indicating that all team members participated in the project
   f. individual memorandums from each team member answering the following question: "What did you learn as a result of participating in this international virtual teamwork project?"

EVALUATION RESULTS

The projects were all completed on schedule. A number of hardships in electronic communication, virtual teamwork, international and cross-cultural working relationships, and project understanding were encountered and mastered. In all cases, the final projects and student efforts far exceeded our expectations. At their own initiatives, for example, students posted their final results on web sites. This added to the bond developed among members of the international teams.

At the end of the project, all students completed the evaluation described in the Appendix. Overall results were very positive and the instructors were strongly encouraged to provide further opportunities for similar project work in the future. It was clear to the instructors that the Thailand projects worked best given their linkage with students taking a parallel course and also being held accountable for project performance as part of their final grades.

We were not able to get final evaluations from the Malaysian participants. Selected results of the evaluation for the Ohio University students and Thailand students follow. The numerical ratings shown in Table 1 suggest that the projects could be considered successful overall while still leaving room for improvement. The open-ended narrative responses that follow provide a variety of insights into project facets.

What Did You Like Most About This Project?

Points of Agreement Between Classes

- Communication within a group and with others around the world.
- Working with others in another country.
- Discovering the differences between two cultures.
- The information exchange.
- Learning about management style outside the class.
- The international virtual team.
- Creating something and putting it on the web.

Unique Points–Ohio University Participants

- Interpreting and theorizing about the data generated.
- The lasting value of the project–the great outcome.
- Working in a team environment, pooling of ideas, high level of input from the team.
- The difficulty/challenge of working with the international team.
- The unique nature of the project.
- Putting it on the Web/computer skills.
- Enjoyed the difficulty and subsequent sense of accomplishment with the final project.

TABLE 1. Evaluation Results for Ohio University and Thailand Teams

Rating Scale: 1 = Very Poor 2 = Poor 3 = Average 4 = Good 5 = Very Good

OU mean (for teams working with Thailand)	Thai mean		
4.4	3.9	A)	The "general" learning value of the project.
4.2	3.8	B)	The value of the project in increased "international" awareness.
4.1	4.2	C)	The value of the project in increased "cross-cultural" understanding.
4.0	4.2	D)	The value of the project in increased competency with computer technology.
4.3	4.0	E)	The value of the project in learning about "face-to-face" teamwork.
4.7	4.3	F)	The value of the project in learning about "computer-mediated" teamwork.
4.6	4.2	G)	The value of the project as a graded assignment in the management course.

Unique Points–Bangkok University Participants

- Learning how culture affects management.
- Internet communication with a foreign country.

What Did You Like Least About This Project?

Points of Agreement Between Classes

- OU's Internet system.
- It was too short.
- Inequality in work distribution within the team.

Unique Points–Ohio University Participants

- I liked it all.
- Too many people in the group.
- The small sample size.
- The team size was too small.
- Getting people to fill out the surveys.
- The time difference limited opportunities for communication.
- Learned very little about the Malaysian culture.
- Not being contacted by the Malaysians; their late participation.

Unique Points–Bangkok University Participants

- Working with BU-Net–it is hard to get on line.

What Are The Most Important Things You Learned from Doing This Project?

Points of Agreement Between Classes

- How American and Thai cultures differed and how people are the same.
- Computer skills.
- Time management.
- Importance of communication within the group and across cultures.
- Learning about survey analysis.
- Computer mediated teamwork.
- International communication.
- Working in a group–allowing for others' needs–dividing the task between team members.

- The importance of other cultures and their needs.

Unique Points–Ohio University Participants

- I took more out of this project than I will ever know.
- The importance of good communication with individuals–electronically and personally.

Unique Points–Bangkok University Participants

- The attitude of Americans doing business.
- How to be a better team member.

DISCUSSION AND FUTURE CONSIDERATIONS

A number of things were learned from this experiment in international virtual teamwork. Perhaps most importantly the authors learned that the project offers high value to the students without high costs from the instructor and/or host institutions. Once the projects were designed and coordinated with our international collaborators and computer support services, the students largely did the rest. And they did that superbly. We believe that many faculty members have opportunities now available for engaging their students in international virtual teamwork. Every international conference that one attends brings new contacts. E-mail is now accessible to virtually everyone, and new group-oriented communication software such as Lotus Domino is becoming more and more available. There is very little direct cost required to set up these projects given the availability of the Internet. Based upon our experience, however, we strongly suggest that international collaborators include the project formally in their own courses and require that students participate for a grade.

In terms of future possibilities and considerations, the following additional open-ended evaluation results offer a variety of student perspectives that can be useful to those who might pursue similar projects.

Would You Recommend That This Project Be Made Available to Other Students in the Future?

Yes 49 No 1

Why or why not?

Points of Agreement Between Classes

- It deals with teamwork, management, and cross-cultural issues.
- It's an opportunity to learn outside the classroom.
- Helps with time management skills.
- Good practice in cross-cultural communication.
- Strengthens cultural awareness and teamwork abilities.
- It is very interesting and you learn a lot while having fun.
- It has helped us recognize the importance of establishing communication on many levels.

Unique Points–Ohio University Participants

- Time consuming but worth it.
- Great international experience to add to your resumé.
- But only if the Malaysians are required to complete the project as part of their grade.
- This project should be worth more in terms of overall points than other projects.

Unique Points–Bangkok University Participants

- Global economic issues are important–helps develop skill for SWOT analysis.

How Would You Change the Project to Make it Better in the Future?

Points of Agreement Between Classes

- Increase the sample size for better accuracy in the assessments.
- Collect more data.
- More time to complete.
- Time to learn more about the individuals.
- Private Lotus Domino accounts for each group and training on software use.

Unique Points–Ohio University Participants

- Create some way to meet the international students we worked with.
- Presentations before a COB board.
- Include the Web page as part of the assignment.

- Increase interaction time for teams.
- More structure–project description and expectations.
- Paired with individuals from another country to circumvent team communication difficulties.
- Assure timely and accurate participation by the other culture.

Unique Points–Bangkok University Participants

- More of a defined research objective and scope.
- Preparation of participants ahead of time.

Use This Space to Share Additional Reactions to the Project and/or Recommendations for Its Future Use.

Points of Agreement Between Classes

- Great improvement in education, but OU needs better Internet support for it to work well.
- Using the same example group for all would be better.
- Students could create the project.
- If more time were given, the project might be started at the beginning of the quarter.
- Earlier start date to get more international participation–the full effect of the project is lost without it.
- Participants should have preliminary background information before the start.
- Emphasize teamwork even more in the future.
- A real time multimedia hook-up would be great during the project.
- Excellent experience, it was well planned and executed.

Unique Points–Ohio University Participants

- Good but needs to be centered on a different topic.
- Group presentations would make project more complete.
- Enjoyed the fact that some freedom was given in determining group. structure and would strongly encourage more in the future.

Unique Points–Bangkok University Participants

- Thank you very much for this experience.
- More feedback from the instructor.

- Expand to include Europe and Japan.
- Make a team from the U.S. and two other countries.

CONCLUSION

Through this experience we have gained the motivation to pursue these projects again in the future. Indeed, we would be pleased to hear from colleagues who would like to join us in similar international virtual teamwork intiatives. We are also encouraged that the students involved will pursue their own international opportunities, both in education and in work. This was recently reinforced when two of the international virtual teamwork participants from the past year enrolled for special summer schools sponsored by our college in Hungary and Spain. Most importantly, this paper is offered in the hope of encouraging others to take advantage of capabilities for engaging their students in interesting and high value-added international virtual teamwork course projects . . . and to share the results of their efforts with others.

REFERENCES

AACSB Newsline. (1998). Virtual campuses offer compelling reasons for business schools to improve their distance vision. Spring: 2-10.

Beck, John, Whiteley, Alma, and McFetridge, Peter. (1996). Internationalising the business student. *Journal of Teaching in International Business*. 7: 91-105.

Boatler, Robert. (1992). World-minded attitude change in a study abroad program: Contact and content issues. *Journal of Teaching in International Business* 3(4): 59-68.

Drucker, Peter F. (1997). Looking ahead: implications of the present. *Harvard Business Review*. September-October, 75: 18-32.

Economist. (1997). Down with distance. September 13.

Galegher, J. and Kraut, R. (1994). Computer-mediated communication for intellectual teamwork: An experiment in group writing. *Information Systems Research*, 5(2): 110-138.

Journal of Teaching in International Business. (1997). Entire issue. 7:4.

Kedia, Ben L. and Cornwell, T. Bettina. (1994). Mission based strategies for internationalizing U.S. business schools. *Journal of Teaching in International Business*, 5(3): 11-29.

Kendall, Kenneth. (1997). The significance of information systems research on emerging technologies: Seven information technologies that promise to improve managerial effectiveness. *Decision Sciences*, 28(4): 775-792.

Kwok, Chuck, Arpan, Jeffrey, and Folds, Jr., William. (1994). A global survey of international business education in the 1990s. *Journal of International Business Studies*. 3: 605-623.

Lewis, L. Floyd. (1996). Using group support systems (GSS) in the teaching of international business. *Journal of Teaching in International Business.* 7(4): 31-47.
Lipnack, Jessica and Stamps, Jeffrey. (1997). *Virtual teams: Reaching across space, time, and organizations with technology.* New York: John Wiley and Sons, Inc.
Oravec, Jo Ann. (1996). *Virtual individuals, virtual groups: Human dimensions of GroupWare and computer networking.* New York, NY: Cambridge University Press.
Orlikowski, Wanda and Hofman, J. Debra. (1997). An improvisational model for change management: The case of GroupWare technologies. *Sloan Management Review.* 38(2) Winter: 11-21.
Schermerhorn, John R., Jr. (1999). *Management,* Sixth Edition. New York: John Wiley & Sons.
Stewart, Thomas A. (1997). *Intellectual Capital: The Wealth of Organizations.* New York: Doubleday.
Wall Street Journal. (1997). Work week. October 28: A1.
Warkentin, Merrill E., Sayeed, Lutfus, and Hightower, Ross. (1997). Virtual teams versus face-to-face teams: An exploratory study of a web-based conference system. *Decision Sciences,* 28(4): 975-996.
Waters, Richard. (1997). Own words: Jack Welch, General Electric. *Financial Times.* October 1.

APPENDIX

Evaluation Questions

MGT300 International Virtual Teamwork Projects

1. Rate the project using the following scales;
   1 = Very Poor
   2 = Poor
   3 = Average
   4 = Good
   5 = Very Good

A._____ The "general" learning value of the project for you.
B._____ The value of the project for you in terms of increased "international" awareness.
C._____ The value of the project for you in terms of increased "cross-cultural" understanding.
D._____ The value of the project for you in terms of increased competency with "computer technology" ultilization.
E._____ The value of the project to you in terms of learning more about "face-to-face teamwork."
F._____ The value of the project to you in terms of learning more about "computer-mediated teamwork."
G._____ The value of the project as a graded assignment on the management course.

2. What did you like MOST about this project?
3. What are the most important things you learned from doing this project?
4. What did you like LEAST about this project?
5. What are the things that you would change to make this a better project for the future?
6. Would you recommend that this project remain an option in the management course?
   Yes No (Circle one)
   Why or why not?
7. This project was made possible in part by a small grant from the Center for International Studies at Ohio University. Based upon your experience in the project, was this project deserving of university support?
   Yes No (Circle one)
   Why or why not?

Crossing the International Teaching Divide–The Evaluation of an Internet Based Teaching Project

Don Scott
Catherine Durnell Cramton
Stéphane Gauvin
Beata Lobert Jones
Gerhard Steinke

SUMMARY. This paper reports the results of a study which examined the use of the Internet as the means by which international business students who were engaged in a collaborative learning project could conduct their interactions at distances of many thousands of miles.

The students were surveyed after completion of the project. The difficulties, which they experienced when using this medium of communication, are reported, as are the positive aspects, which were identified. The survey also identified key areas of suggested improvement for

---

Don Scott is Professor of Management in the School of Commerce and Management, Southern Cross University. Catherine Durnell Cramton is Assistant Professor, Management in the Graduate Business Institute, George Mason University. Stéphane Gauvin is Associate Professor and Head of the Department of Marketing, Université Laval. Beata Lobert Jones is Assistant Professor in the Neeley School of Business, Texas Christian University and Gerhard Steinke is Associate Professor of Management and Information Systems in the School of Business and Economics, Seattle Pacific University.

The authors wish to thank the anonymous referees for their comments and suggestions which have been incorporated into this paper.

[Haworth co-indexing entry note]: "Crossing the International Teaching Divide–The Evaluation of an Internet Based Teaching Project." Scott, Don et al. Co-published simultaneously in *Journal of Teaching in International Business* (The International Business Press, an imprint of The Haworth Press, Inc.) Vol. 10, No. 3/4, 1999, pp. 61-79; and: *Teaching and Program Variations in International Business* (ed: Erdener Kaynak and John R. Schermerhorn, Jr.) The International Business Press, an imprint of The Haworth Press, Inc., 1999, pp. 61-79. Single or multiple copies of this article are available for a fee from The Haworth Document Delivery Service [1-800-342-9678, 9:00 a.m. - 5:00 p.m. (EST). E-mail address: getinfo@haworthpressinc.com].

future Internet based collaborative projects.

The paper discusses the results of the study and suggests methods by which Internet based teaching projects can be improved, as well as areas for further research. *[Article copies available for a fee from The Haworth Document Delivery Service: 1-800-342-9678. E-mail address: getinfo@haworthpressinc.com <Website: http://www.haworthpressinc.com>]*

INTRODUCTION

Distance communication methods such as video and telephone conferencing have been used for distance education purposes for a number of years and even today are being proposed for more extended use (Feller, 1995; Lucas 1996; Winner, 1994). However, experiences at some universities have shown them to have had limited success.[1]

The advent of the Internet and the World Wide Web (WWW) has introduced new distance communication possibilities to the educational community (Duguet, 1995). However, much of the value of this medium has arisen from the potential for greater levels of communication between academics and post-graduate students particularly in terms of their ongoing research. This has taken place either via direct communication or by being members of listserv-based discussion groups (for example, those for marketing, e.g., ELMAR, services marketing, e.g., SERVNET, and statistical methodologies, e.g., SEMNET). Many listserv groups exist for discussions in a multitude of fields such as human behaviour, psychology, statistics, computer usages, etc.

Some existing educational organisations with on-campus students and distance programs have already begun to take advantage of the existence of the Internet by providing on-line lecture notes and course materials for their on-campus and distance education students (Vasarhelji and Graham, 1997). Bjorner (1993) has provided details of on-line course offerings available through computers and modems. Moskowitz (1995) has been able to detail more than 70 colleges and universities who are trying to make their regular course offerings available on-line, and Velsmid (1997) has supplied recent details of such college and university courses. Businesses such as the Royal

---

1. Discussions with teachers who have used this medium for a number of years at Southern Cross University, Australia and with teachers who have tried the method at other universities have indicated that even with detailed preparation and careful procedural controls to remove the "talking head" syndrome, this method does not cause students to feel that they have had a satisfactory educational experience and that telephonic communications without the video component achieve the same ends. Siedel as quoted in Lucas (1996) also mentions that the normal professor and student interaction is found to be missing when video conferencing is used.

Bank in Canada are also beginning to use the internet for their training programs (Grantham, 1997). However, such training largely relates to the provision of on-line materials and multimedia resources (Horowitz, 1997).

Web pages detailing university facilities, course details and methods of application for course entry is widespread and virtually universally used by most tertiary academic institutions around the world.

The advantage of Internet communication is its ability to span vast distances almost instantaneously and to bring together people from distant areas that may never come face-to-face with one another. In so doing, it is able to provide access to skills that might otherwise have been removed from some of the communicants and to bring into close verbal contact people from different language and cultural backgrounds. One such use is detailed by Chadwick (1995). It provides examples of students from distant educational institutions being able to access data, pictures and web pages in respect to particular educational projects.

Computer-based linkages such as those that are achievable through direct interaction whether by keyboard entry or voice communication, have offered the potential to develop virtual universities. Here, students can meet in virtual surroundings, scan bulletin boards and discuss topics with one another. Virtual universities and on-line campuses offering fully on-line courses have thus begun to make offers to students and details of some of the first of these have been given by Di Lorenzo (1994), Moskowitz (1995) and Velsmid (1997). Internet based technology with virtual interactions, therefore, also offers opportunities for universities to harness new levels of interaction for their students particularly in the field of cross-cultural interactions.

BUSINESS AND THE INTERNET

The world is moving inexorably towards a single global market, and those companies that will survive and prosper particularly in the manufacturing areas in the future, will be those that can adopt a global approach. They will need to set up their businesses in order to harness the benefits of operations or sections of operations in different parts of the world. The ability to do this requires business people to have a good understanding of different cultures. They should be able to interact through the medium of the English language. This is rapidly assuming the role as the major language medium for interchange between countries and according to Cornish (1996) ". . . may become the native language of most people around the world."

Cornish (1996) has also identified a number of ways in which technology will change our lives in the future. In these scenarios he sketches out the situation where telecommunications reduce distances so that "People thousands of miles apart are now finding ways to work together, buy things from each other, and form groups for common purpose." He therefore suggests that, "We are moving towards an era when individuals and organisations will operate almost as if national boundaries and natural boundaries did not separate them." In addition, in the educational field he suggests that "Global universities will emerge, connecting students, lecturers and researchers in many nations via computer networks, satellite television, and other advances."

The New World, which is envisaged by Cornish, may or may not develop to the extent that he has predicted. However, there is no doubt that current levels of information technology already offer the potential for university lecturers to provide greater value for their students. This is particularly in respect of providing them with a better understanding of the capacity of the technology and of people in distant lands and different cultures, aspects of particular importance when teaching international business. An understanding of the potential of the medium will also be essential for future business people if as is suggested by Rogers (1996) there is a ". . . shift towards virtual networked organisations that transcend conventional boundaries."

THE USE OF THE INTERNET FOR TEACHING

However, use of the Internet and WWW in teaching is yet in its infancy. Very few studies have been conducted to examine the difficulties that are likely to be encountered when using this medium for student group instructional interactions. There has also been little research to identify the type or nature of difficulties that will need to be addressed when using the medium.

Vasarhelyi and Graham (1997) have outlined the potential ways in which electronic linkages can be used in teaching. Ives (1996) presented a scenario of the effect of the Internet on business education. He postulated a requirement for radical changes in business structure to combat the rise of other suppliers of education while assuming that personalised instruction from educators will remain a major role although as facilitator or coach rather than as expert. This, however, need not be the case and the level of involvement and type of involvement of instructors is yet to be decided. It will only become apparent as more experience and knowledge is gained about the operation of Internet-based teaching and the student's reaction to the system.

Halal and Layabouts (1994) examined the future impact of electronic communications and multi-media on education and suggested a number of ways in which these systems would impact on education in the future. They also identified a number of universities that were already experimenting with the different media.

From this, it would seem that the use of electronic communications will become more frequent in the future. Hence, investigations of the difficulties to be overcome when using these media and of areas of focus for delivery of optimum results for students are urgently required.

A few studies have also been carried out to examine the possibilities inherent in using the Internet as a teaching medium (Atwong, Lange, Doak and Aijo, 1996; O'Brien, 1996). These studies have reported on some of the effects/difficulties encountered by the instructors such as the need to train students in the technology, differences in approach between students from different cultural backgrounds and matching of times. However, there have not been detailed student evaluations of the process and its difficulties. If educational organisations are to be able to constructively improve their utilisation of the new technologies of distance communication it is essential that the problems and barriers encountered by students in utilising the new technology be carefully researched. This paper has conducted and reports on an evaluation by international students after they had been involved in an Internet-based collaborative distance learning exercise.

THE NATURE OF THE STUDY

Collaborative learning is that which involves interpersonal processes whereby a small group of students works together on a specific project. In this form of interaction, learning takes place through discussion and the sharing of information (Leidner and Jarvenpaa, 1995). It has been identified as developing problem solving skills and critical thinking as well as enhancing student satisfaction (Alavi, 1994) and as being superior to individualistic instruction in many areas (Leidner and Jarvenpaa, 1995). It is a common method of instruction in many university courses and it was used as the basis for this study.

The study addressed several of the research issues highlighted by Leidner and Jarvenpaa (1995). These were the exploration of teamwork interactions across global student bodies and the requirements of students and teachers who might interact through the medium of the new communication technologies, when using collaborative learning.

Groups of between 4 and six English speaking MBA or equivalent students from three continents were set a task of developing a business plan for an Internet based product or service offering. While all the students were able to interact in English, not all of them used English as their home language.

A similar project would commonly be carried out in an MBA program with teams operating in an on-campus face-to-face mode. However, the students in this project were placed into their teams with at least two students from the same university teaming up with other pairs of students from other universities. The students were directed to use the Internet in order to interact with their distance team members and were encouraged to engage in direct contact and discussion through the medium of chat-lines as well as through the medium of e-mail.

The students were informed of the educational goals of the project which were to:

- promote active learning in diverse virtual teams and to develop an appreciation of electronic media, team interaction and learning-to-learn issues
- foster critical/integrative knowledge building in the areas of electronic commerce, electronic communities and virtual organisations (including the enabling role of IT)
- further students' learning about the Internet's capabilities for retrieving and communicating information as well as providing resources to support creative decision-making processes.

The study had some similarities to the study by Atwong, Lange, Doak and Aijo (1996), where teams of students from California State University–Fullerton and Lappeenranta University of Technology, Finland carried out a collaborative marketing exercise. However, the report on this study provides only limited information. There is no evidence of an in-depth survey of the students having been carried out in order to gain an overview of the problems and practices that need to be addressed when using the Internet for teaching.

PROJECT DETAILS

Nine universities participated in the project. These universities were: Central Missouri State University, East Carolina University, George Mason University, Seattle Pacific University and Texas Christian University in the USA, The Memorial University of Newfoundland and Université Laval in Canada, Universidade do Minho in Portugal and Southern Cross University in Australia. The number of participants from each university, the courses that were being studied and the numbers of participating students are shown in Table 1.

The teams were made up to include at least one pair of students from one of the US universities with a pair of students from a university located in another country. Non-US partners were located in Australia, Canada and Portugal. There were 45 teams in all. The students ranged in age from 23 to 48 and all were graduate students taking business or management information systems courses. Because some of the students were studying in a different country to their home country, the countries of origin of the students included Canada, Colombia, Germany, Hong Kong, India, Indonesia, Portugal, Thailand, Ukraine and the USA. The study, therefore, examined the interactions between students from a wide range of different cultures. All of

TABLE 1. Student Participant and Respondent Numbers by Country, University and Study Subject

University	Country	Subject being studied	Number of students participating	Number of students responding to the questionnaire
Central Missouri State University	USA	Management Information Systems	15	1
East Carolina University	USA	Core Management Information Systems	6	4
George Mason University	USA	Leveraging Information Technology	26	12
Seattle Pacific University	USA	Introduction to Information Systems	8	6
Texas Christian University	USA	Core Information Systems	93	7
The Memorial University of Newfoundland	Canada	Core Information Systems	24	8
Université Laval	Canada	Marketing and Management of Technology	19	19
Universidade do Minho	Portugal	Information Systems	10	4
Southern Cross University	Australia	Strategic Management	12	12

the students who were based in Australia, were Asian students who were studying there on a one-year postgraduate study program.

The project was set out on the WWW at a VLE (virtual learning environment) project site at http://zeta.is.tcu.edu/~blobert/vle/project.html. The Information, which was provided, on these web pages introduced the students to the project. It gave them a background and informed them of the requirements for the project as perceived by the various staff members who were supervising the different classes at the different universities. The pages also identified the different members of each team who had been chosen to work together so that participants could look up their own name and find their fellow team members.

A suggested method of proceeding with the project was also set out. Members were encouraged to engage in early Internet based familiarisation sessions with their team members, and could also use a web site to determine their personality type using a Jungian based system of classification.

The task, which was set, was that the students should produce an international business plan for an Internet based business. This business would offer a product or service world wide, via the WWW. It would present the plan via the Internet to a theoretical Web Venture Capital Group that might be interested in funding the venture. The students were provided with an outline format for the international business plan and with the assessment criteria. The experiment operated successfully in that all the student groups did return at least reasonable projects. However, in a few instances team disagreements resulted in some team members independently returning their own different projects since they were not in full agreement with the group project outcome.

Examination of transcripts of discussions in the case of one of the teams which encountered major disagreements, revealed a situation where initial disharmony was fostered as a result of tardy early link-ups by overseas team members with their USA team members. This resulted in comments being made by the USA team members to the effect that the project would be easier if the distant partners never came on board. Further difficulties then appeared to have developed because of cultural differences, where lack of disagreement by the overseas team members led to the USA students assuming that agreement had been reached. In fact, this was not the situation since the cultural background of the overseas students meant that they perceived outright disagreement to unacceptable behaviour. They therefore continued to proffer alternate suggestions which caused extreme irritation amongst the USA team members, who felt that these were irrelevant suggestions. Eventual final communication breakdown occurred further down the track when the overseas students seemed to have overcome some of their cultural inhibitions and burst out with messages stating that they had never agreed to the project in the first place.

On completion of the project, the students were surveyed via an Internet survey form to evaluate the team interaction processes and their learning experience. Seventy-three responses were received. Table 1 also details the number of responses by university.

NATURE OF COMMUNICATION METHODS USED

The participants in the experiment had a number of possible methods of communicating with one another and Table 2 details the nature and frequency of communication that was reported. It is apparent that the greatest amount of contact was occasioned by face-to-face meetings with local team members. In relation to the distance communication component, e-mail was the most used communication method followed by the chat lines.

Some students such as those in Australia experienced great difficulty in

TABLE 2. Nature and Frequency of Respondents' Contacts During the Project

Contact type	None	1-5	6-20	21+	Don't know
Face-to-face meetings with local partners	8	18	33	13	1
Phone calls to local partner	8	22	35	8	0
Phone calls to virtual partner	48	21	3	1	0
Faxes sent	50	22	1	0	0
Faxes received	62	11	0	0	0
E-mail items sent	0	3	28	42	0
E-mail items received	0	2	27	42	2
Hours on chat lines	14	29	27	1	2
Minutes on video link	72	0	0	0	1

using the chat lines. This was both as a result of a lack of local expertise and the fact that the lines from Australia were insufficient to handle the amount of traffic required and hence tended to break down reasonably frequently. These students therefore tended to use e-mail to a major extent. However, this did not explain the frequency of e-mail communication that was evidenced by most of the respondent students. It would seem that e-mail was found a very useful means of distance communication in a team situation. This was the case for those students who were interacting with fellow team members within the same country as well as for those in other countries.

Evaluation of Project Aspects

The students were asked to state whether they agreed or disagreed with a number of statements relating to the project overall as a learning exercise and the process which they had employed in working as virtual teams. The responses to these questions are listed in Table 3 in terms of the respondents' agreement or disagreement with the statements.

The percentages listed add to less than 100 in each case because of the non-reflection of the responses by those students who neither agreed nor disagreed with the statements. In order to identify those issues where there was a clear majority either in agreement or disagreement with a statement, z values were calculated.The difference between the different proportions of agreement and disagreement and were then corrected to allow for the increased chance of the occurrence of a Type I error. This might have arisen because of the repeated nature of assessment of the answers to the questions.

Examination of those questions where a significant orientation towards

TABLE 3. Respondents' Views on Project Aspects

Project aspect	Percentage disagree	Percentage agree	z-value
Teamwork			
All team members did their best	27.4	67.1	4.8**
Our team worked well	28.8	63.0	4.1**
Local partners more helpful than virtual ones	28.8	43.8	1.9
Local team members did more work than virtual partners	38.4	26.0	1.6
Defining member roles was easy	27.4	63.0	4.3**
Business plan style			
Really proud of our plan	15.1	65.8	6.2**
Could not have done this plan on my own	35.6	45.2	1.1
Comparison of Real and Virtual Teams			
Virtual teams more efficient than face-to-face teams	71.2	8.2	7.8**
Virtual teams more efficient than anticipated	38.4	42.5	0.5
Virtual teams more fun than face-to-face teams	45.2	24.7	2.6
Virtual teams more fun than anticipated	34.2	47.9	1.7
Success/Failure Factors			
Time pressure increases the likelihood of success in a virtual environment	41.1	37.0	0.5
Familiarity with Internet technologies a key success factor	8.2	83.6	9.1**
Cultural similarity a key ingredient for success in virtual environments	45.2	27.4	2.2
Participant's personality a key factor for success in virtual environments	12.3	79.5	8.1**
Overall project evaluation			
Went better than expected	24.7	52.1	3.4*
Would do it again	8.2	83.6	9.1**
Would prefer local teams to virtual teams for the same or similar task	35.6	34.2	0.2
Would prefer to work alone rather than in virtual teams	65.7	13.7	6.4**

* Significant at the 95% level after Bonferroni correction
** Significant at the 99% level after Bonferroni correction

either agreement or disagreement existed yielded a number of interesting observations.

Overall, the responding students were positively oriented towards their teams. There was a majority view that the teams had worked well, that choosing member roles was easy, that all members did their best and that they were proud of their plan. This would indicate that virtual teams can produce beneficial team results. Hence, the use of virtual teams in international business teaching situations can enhance the learning experience even though some of the members do not come into face-to-face contact with one another. This view is further supported by the fact that a predominance of respondents also felt that they would prefer to work in virtual teams rather than alone.

However, there is a possibility that the responses were biased towards those team members who felt positively about the virtual team exercise. The non-respondents could have constituted students who did not feel that the experience had been beneficial and hence that the positive aspects of the virtual team experience was not experienced by the majority of the students. Even if this were to be the case, it would not detract from the fact that some students can produce a positive team feeling when working in virtual teams. It would highlight the need to identify the possible problem areas that can arise with virtual teams. In this regard the areas of difficulty identified by the largely positive body of respondents would be even more important as they would identify very key areas of required concentration when conducting teaching exercises using virtual teams.

Inspection of the other areas of majority opinion showed that the respondent students felt that knowledge of Internet technology was of importance as was the participant's personality. Although the responses did not show a significant consensus for either agreement or disagreement, there was a suggestion that a majority of the respondent students might have felt that cultural similarity was not important. However, in the light of the recorded interactions described earlier, cultural differences may have played a major role in some instances and may be particular to certain types of cultural differences. There was also a suggestion that the virtual aspect of the team exercise detracted from the experience they might have had in a face-to-face situation.

The conclusion to be drawn from these results would be that any students who are to engage in an Internet-based virtual learning exercise should be well trained in regards to the use of the technology. The training of the people in the teams is also an important issue to overcome both virtual interaction and cultural differences. It would seem possible that distance-based team interactions will require that more attention is paid to team building than in the case of face-to-face teams. This could be because of the lack of direct contact and the absence of body language in the interactions. However, this was not able to be assessed in this study and represents an area for future research. The nature of and effect of different cultural aspects on virtual interactions is also an area requiring further research.

A distance-based method of interaction does evidence a potential for enhanced problems with team disagreements and there is a need for careful team training and the provision of tools to help manage team dynamics. It is also evident that more training about the challenges of dispersed teamwork is needed, when using distance-based teams for instructional purposes.

SIGNIFICANT FEATURES OF THE VIRTUAL TEAM EXPERIENCE

Using interval-scaled responses from the respondent students, the data was examined for significant associations using multiple regression to examine two models. The first model depicted the association between the scoring of the statement "It went generally better than anticipated" and a number of features of the team interaction experience. The overall model was found to be supported by the data ($p = 0.0001$). A subsequent stepwise regression with entry and exit levels set at $p = 0.05$ was then used to identify the significant variables. The results of this regression analysis are shown in Table 4.

The significant variables mainly related to team interactions and it would seem that the respondents' perception of better than expected performance was linked to the level of positive team interaction. It should be noted that the coefficient for "local team did more work than our virtual partners," was negative. Hence, the level of positive appreciation was in part linked to team members finding that the contribution of the distant team members was equal to that of the local team members. Other interesting aspects were that there was a positive association with the concept that virtual teams were more efficient than face-to-face teams and that pressure was seen to increase the likelihood of success in a virtual environment. It would seem possible that this latter association was because pressure increased the rate of response by virtual team members and that communication was an important ingredient in team success.

TABLE 4. Model 1 Stepwise Regression Results

Dependent variable: "It went generally better than anticipated"

Variable	Coefficient	p > F
Worked as a real team	0.28	0.0003
Virtual teams more efficient than anticipated	0.26	0.0023
Local team did more work than our virtual partners	−0.22	0.0016
Virtual teams more efficient than face-to-face teams	0.21	0.0367
More time pressure increases the likelihood of success in a virtual environment	0.18	0.0046

$R^2 = 0.70$

The second model depicted the relationship between "our team worked as a real team" and the team interaction features. The overall model was again supported by the data (p = 0.0001). A subsequent stepwise regression with entry and exit levels set at p = 0.05 was used to identify the significant variables. The results of this regression analysis are shown in Table 5.

The positive assessment of team performance was seen to be mainly associated with a perception that all team members had done their best and with a better than expected level of virtual team efficiency. It would appear that the fact that the respondents were "really proud of our plan" might have influenced their perception of the performance of the team. However, this association could also be because when teams felt that they had worked well they were also more proud of their final output.

It was noted that in the case of both models, "defining roles went relatively easily" was positively associated with the project going better than anticipated and the respondents' teams working as a "real team." It would seem likely that, where teams interacted well from the start, or where the team members brought different required skills to the team, and hence contributed perceivable value to the team effort, there would have been little conflict over the roles of the different team members. However, this possibility was not assessed in this study and therefore represents an area for further research.

PROJECT MEMBERS' LIKES AND DISLIKES

The information and analysis conducted above provided some information in respect of areas of evaluation that could be easily identified. Because of the very new nature of the method of instruction, however, it was very likely that this information could have overlooked particular issues of importance. It might also not have identified the real reasons lying behind responses to the

TABLE 5. Model 2 Stepwise Regression Results

Dependent variable: "Our team worked as a real team"

Variable	Coefficient	p > F
Everyone did his/her best	0.50	0.0001
Virtual teams more efficient than anticipated	0.30	0.0001
Really proud of our plan	0.19	0.0072
Defining roles went relatively easily	0.14	0.0001

$R^2 = 0.77$

closed questions. For this reason, the respondents were also asked to list the three features of the project that they liked most and the three features that they liked least. These open responses were then inspected and grouped into categories, which appeared to best represent the key aspects relating to the different responses. Table 6 lists the categories identified and the frequency of response in respect of the most liked project features.

The most-liked features of the project related to those areas of learning which were intended to be developed, namely knowledge about the Internet and the technology that is used to access the features of the Internet and team relationships. The Internet knowledge comments were expressed in statements such as: "A better knowledge of Internet technology," "connecting members of different countries," "creating a web page" and "experience of working on Internet." Another major area was the knowledge of other peoples and cultures. These were expressed in terms of statements such as "interacting with people from a different environment"; "got a taste of different cultures"; "getting to know people with diverse backgrounds"; "country interaction"; "cultural difference"; "interacting with students from outside of (sic) my school." Another main area of liking was related to experiences with individual and team relationships. These were expressed in terms of comments such as the following. "Access to teams from other schools"; "Enteracting (sic) with my Virtual Team Members"; "It forced me to work with people I wouldn't have"; "Having the challenge of motivating those you are not in face-to-face contact with"; "New Experience in working together."

In addition, students also enjoyed the novelty of the experience ("excitement of a new experience"; "New learning experience"; "Sounds like a cutting edge project"). They felt that they had acquired business skills from the nature and content of the projects ("real project"; "creating a business plan for an exciting product"; "It was a great experience and the business plan was a good idea for that"). They also felt that they had acquired skills in

TABLE 6. Most Liked Aspects of the Project

Project aspect	Number of mentions
Internet knowledge and skills	66
Interactions with other cultures and people	47
Individual and team relationships	30
Developing business skills	17
New and novel experiences	14
Enhancement of efficiency	10
Interesting and challenging experience	7
Freedom of project format	2

regard to the application of the Internet to business practice ("Application of a 'real' business via the Internet" and "I learned a lot about businesses on the Internet, it would not be that hard to start up something on the Internet").

The most disliked features of the project are listed in Table 7.

A wider range of disliked features was apparent with the most frequently mentioned dislikes relating to problems that were experienced with using the technology to communicate. These were grouped into a number of different categories. By far the most disliked features of the projects were those that could be categorised as team interaction problems. These were expressed in terms of phrases such as: "Conflicts amongst members," "distribution of work (Very Hard)" and "difficult to solve problems if one has differences with one's virtual team members."

This result, while obviously a source of real concern to the team members, did however identify the fact that the distance-separated teams had experienced team interactions. The primary difficulty that they had experienced meant that although the team members were separated by distance their learning experience did encompass the problems of dealing in-group interactive situations with other team members. This was an intended aspect of the project experience.

The second most disliked category of project features was related to communications difficulties, for example "Communication limitations" and "Communication difficulties resulting from no face-to-face meetings." Next were technology faults and technological inadequacies such as "Dependence on technology–if something went wrong it set us back," "Difficult to get through on chat lines–was unsuccessful" and "freezing of computers while

TABLE 7. Most Disliked Aspects of the Project

Project aspect	Number of mentions
Team interaction difficulties	41
Technological inadequacies	27
Communication difficulties	25
Time pressures	22
Different university requirements	17
Project organisation/co-ordination	16
Inadequate prior knowledge	8
Technological faults	6
Time zone problems	8
Technical support	5
Slowness of interaction via the internet	4
Poor project outcomes	3
Lack of privacy	2
Cultural/language problems	2

working." These difficulties related in part to the as yet quite early stage of development of internet communications, in particular, the chat lines and to the overloading of lines between some countries such as Australia and the USA.

Project co-ordination problems and different university requirements were other identified problems. These could be ascribed to the fact that the project universities operated on different times and were involved in teaching different subjects. This highlighted a need for future projects to be conducted by teams from classes which were studying the same subject material and to a need to set up a project timetable which is compatible with all the participating universities' courses. This problem was also highlighted by another disliked feature namely time pressures. It would appear that the project was too substantial for completion within the time allowed, while at the same time allowing for the need to acquire the Internet communication skills required and to develop the team understanding needed. It would appear that a necessary activity prior to future projects of this nature would be the use of preparatory exercises. These would enable the teams to get to know one another and to gain facility with using the Internet and the communications media.

ADDITIONAL SUGGESTIONS FOR IMPROVEMENT WHEN USING INTERNET BASED PROJECTS

Students were also asked to make suggestions as to the ways in which similar projects could best be improved in the future. These comments essentially addressed the elements of the project, which had already been identified in terms of the most disliked aspects. Their categorised responses are shown in Table 8.

In this table, the major suggestions related to project aspects that students obviously perceived as being directly under control of the project organiser(s). Thus, two of the primary suggestions related to better co-ordination of the project across participant universities, particularly in terms of assessment standards and project requirements and clearer guidelines for project participants. Typical comments in this regard were "all locations have identical requirements," "all students should have the same deliverables," "develop consistency between professors' criteria and deadlines." More time for the project was also seen to be an important requirement, a typical comment being "A longer time frame to complete the project." A requirement for prior training in the technology as typified by the comment, "The students must already be familiar with e-mail and web browsers" was also identified as an area for potential improvement. A pleasing aspect of the comments was the suggestion for a requirement for more team building exercises prior to the

TABLE 8. Suggested Project Improvements

Project aspect	Number of mentions
Better co-ordination across universities	36
More training on the technology prior to the project	30
More emphasis on team building and teamwork facilitation	27
More time for the project	23
Clearer guidelines and direction	23
Better communications links	20
Task tailored to suit all team members	5
Better technical support	3
Improved equipment	2

project (for example, "Create exercises up front to build team cohesion"). This reflected the fact that, as intended, the project had proved in many instances to identify the types of problems that are often encountered in team situations. However, it is also an area of focus that should be taken into account when conducting similar exercises.

A requirement for better communications links, improved technology and technical support reflected the fact that the Internet is not yet an ideal communications medium and that its use can cause communications problems. It is expected that this situation will change over the next five years as the linkages and technology improves.

CONCLUSIONS

The major conclusions that can be drawn from this study can be summarised as follows:

Teams comprised of distance separated members can operate reasonably as teams by using the Internet as a communications medium even when separated by major distances and incorporating people from different countries and cultures. Some teams returned very good joint efforts. There were a few instances of major team disagreements resulting in individual team members separately handing in different project returns. However, these were few in numbers and possibly did not exceed the normal level of team disagreements that are commonly encountered with face-to-face teams. Although there is a suggestion from the qualitative information that some cultural differences may cause difficulties, there is no evidence that this would be any different than in face-to-face team interactions.

The Internet is not yet fully suitable for distance based team members to be able to achieve optimum levels of possible benefit from their collaboration. This is because of the problems that can currently be encountered with the bandwidth of distance communications and in particular with the chat lines (Horowitz, 1997). It is to be expected that Internet advances around the world will lead to better and better communications possibilities as time progresses. However, the rapid rate of increase in Internet traffic expected in the immediate future may cause a short-term deterioration in communications capabilities.

Because of the current attenuation of communications as a result of Internet usage, teams comprised of distance separated members should allow longer times for team members to become acquainted with one another than would be anticipated with face-to-face teams. This additional time should be arranged prior to the commencement of the project work. Prior training of team members and experience of such members with the use of communications software is required. The concurrent elimination of any technological teething problems is also an essential requirement when using teams comprised of distance separated team members linked by Internet based communication.

The project exercise used in this trial, incorporated students who were studying a number of different courses. It is evident that it would be more satisfactory if future exercises were to link students with similar academic or experiential backgrounds who were studying the same subject material in similar courses with common evaluation criteria.

When teaching internationally, some allowance will also be necessary in order to overcome the problems that are occasioned by universities in different parts of the world operating on different term dates. Universities in different countries are unlikely to change to operate on the same term dates in the near future. It may therefore be necessary for projects, which link teams across different countries to arrange at particular universities for the project to operate outside normal term dates so that all team members can have the same deadlines.

In the business area, some businesses are already using intranets to communicate across the world and these are likely to be more and more used for international business team interactions. It is anticipated that such interactions will probably experience similar effects to those identified through this project. These are likely to be very evident if they link people who have not previously met and who come from dissimilar backgrounds and cultures, into team activities. As identified, in this research there will need to be sufficient time allowed for electronically linked team members to firstly become acquainted with each other before commencing any team activities. The use of team building exercises would be recommended during this phase. Even in those instances where team members have already met in face-to-face situations and/or already know the other team members it will be necessary to make allowances for the communications difficulties. These can arise from interacting through a medium which removes much of the normal social interaction aspects of teamwork and interactive communication elements such as body language, facial expressions, etc. However, this research indicates that internet linked teams can be efficient and can provide an enjoyable experience for the members. This suggests that there is a potential for considerable future savings in the area of team interactions for international businesses.

REFERENCES

Alavi, Maryam. (1994). Computer-mediated collaborative learning: An empirical evaluation. *MIS Quarterly*, 18(2): 159-174.

Atwong, Catherine T., Lange, Irene L., Doak, Les and Aijo, Toivo S. (1996). How collaborative learning spans the globe. *Marketing News*, 30(17):16,19.

Bjorner. (1993). The virtual college classroom. *Link-up*, 10(4):21-23.

Chadwick, John. (1995). How learning is aided by technology. *Link-up*, 12(1):16.

Cornish, Edward. (1996). The cyber future: 92 ways our lives will change by the year 2025. *Futurist*, 30(1): SS1-SS15.

Di Lorenzo, Jim. (1994). Virtual university born on the internet. *Telephony*, 227(4): 16

Duguet, Pierre. (1995). Education: face-to-face or distance? *Oecd Observer*, (194):17-20.

Feller, Gordon. (1995). University of the world. *Communications International*, 22(3):20-23.

Grantham, Tim. (1997). Canadian bank uses multimedia to train employees. *Computerworld*, 31(4):63-65.

Halal, William E. and Jay Layabouts. (1994). Telelearning: The multimedia revolution in education. *Futurist*, 28(6): 21-26.

Horowitz, Alan, S. (1997). Net train, net gain? *Computerworld*, 31(5):63-66.

Ives, Blake. (1996). Will the internet revolutionize business education and research. *Sloan Management Review*, 37(3): 33-41.

Leidner, Dorothy E. and Sirkka L. Jarvenpaa. (1995). The use of information technology to enhance management school education. *MIS Quarterly*, 19(3): 265-291.

Lucas, Allison. (1996). A virtual business degree. *Sales and Marketing Management*, 148(3):14.

Moskowitz, Robert. (1995). Distance education. *Link-up*, 12(6):38-40.

Rogers, Debra M Amidon. (1996). The challenge of the fifth generation R&D. *Research Technology Management*, 39(4) 33-41.

Vasarhelji, Miklos A. and Lynford Graham. (1997). Cybersmart: education and the internet. *Management Accounting*, August:32-36.

Velsmid, Debra A. (1997). The electronic classroom. *Link-Up*, 14(1):32-33.

Winner, Langdon. (1994). The virtually educated. *Technology Review*, 97(4):66.

Organizational Learning and Market Orientation in International Marketing Education

G. Tomas M. Hult
Bruce D. Keillor

SUMMARY. This study develops and tests a series of relationships between organizational learning and market orientation as it pertains to international marketing education. The focus is on the activities and relationships between the students, faculty, and staff in the international marketing/business program at three schools in the north, midwest, and south United States. Based on a sample of 193 undergraduate and graduate international marketing students, the results suggest that organizational learning (class and major area-based learning)–team orientation, systems orientation, learning orientation, and memory orientation–positively influences market orientation learning outcomes (i.e., intelligence generation, intelligence dissemination, and responsiveness). The major implication of the study is that the education provided to the students in an international marketing course (i.e., upper-division university course) can be enhanced by focusing on organizational learning tools as a means to increase the shared knowledge level among the students. *[Article copies available for a fee from The Haworth Document*

G. Tomas M. Hult, PhD, is Director of International Business and Assistant Professor of Marketing and International Business, College of Business, Florida State University, Tallahassee, FL 32306-1110 (E-mail: thult@cob.fsu.edu).

Bruce D. Keillor, PhD, is Assistant Professor of Marketing and International Business, College of Business Administration, Southwest Missouri State University, Springfield, MO 65804-0094 (E-mail: bdk877f@vma.smsu.edu).

[Haworth co-indexing entry note]: "Organizational Learning and Market Orientation in International Marketing Education." Hult, G. Tomas M. and Bruce D. Keillor. Co-published simultaneously in *Journal of Teaching in International Business* (The International Business Press, an imprint of The Haworth Press, Inc.) Vol. 10, No. 3/4, 1999, pp. 81-97; and: *Teaching and Program Variations in International Business* (ed: Erdener Kaynak and John R. Schermerhorn, Jr.) The International Business Press, an imprint of The Haworth Press, Inc., 1999, pp. 81-97. Single or multiple copies of this article are available for a fee from The Haworth Document Delivery Service [1-800-342-9678, 9:00 a.m. - 5:00 p.m. (EST). E-mail address: getinfo@haworthpressinc.com].

Delivery Service: 1-800-342-9678. E-mail address: getinfo@haworthpressinc.com <Website: http://www.haworthpressinc.com>]

The movement to transform organizations to reflect "processes of learning, behavior change, and performance improvement" (Slater and Narver, 1995, p. 63-64) is gaining worldwide momentum. Organizations as diverse as Federal Express, Xerox, CIGNA Insurance, General Motors, and Honda, to mention a few, are reconfiguring organizational charts and management practices to stress organizational learning for the purpose of obtaining a competitive advantage. For example, Federal Express found that becoming a learning organization helped boost the intellectual capital of its sales force (Dumaine 1994). Major Federal Express customers say that the organization's salespeople are much more attuned to customer needs. Employees do not jump to conclusions so readily, are more willing to hear a customer out, and understand customers' dilemmas better after attending seminars and workshops on organizational learning.

Many institutions of higher education also continuously revise and update their teaching methods, faculty structure, and curricula to provide students with an education that will position them for success in a variety of situations and career endeavors. For example, undergraduate and master-level business education is increasingly focusing on team-based approaches to learning. Such learning endeavors stress the students' team orientation, and perhaps most importantly, the notion that a synergy effect can be gained by being learning-oriented at the team (organizational) level. Organizational (class and study program-based) learning as opposed to individual (student) learning becomes most apparent at the senior and graduate levels. In these upper-division courses, the material is often covered by the use of case studies and computer simulations (e.g., Intopia, Markstrat) as a substitute of or in conjunction with the more traditional lecture format. As such, the achieved learning in upper division courses often depend on the "shared knowledge" level of the students in the class due to the more group-oriented instructional methods. This means that by increasing the shared knowledge level among the students in a class, the education provided to all students will be enhanced. For example, as is the case in the samples studied, many international marketing courses have students from a wide variety of countries; it would be detrimental to the value of learning not to involve those students in the structured learning process to share their opinions and experiences. Similarly, the simple interaction between students (and for that managers from around the world in the same company) is a powerful tool when it comes to the micro-level portion of international marketing education.

The objective of this paper is to examine the effects of organizational learning on education-driven market orientation in international marketing education. International marketing courses are often designed as case and/or simulation courses since the topic area lends itself to application-oriented exercises where students can apply theories learned in basic marketing and international business courses. While several other courses and programs would benefit from the "learning organization" framework, we believe that the value of international marketing/business education can be significantly increased by adopting this approach because of the constantly evolving issues that have to be addressed in such learning environments due to the turbulent international marketplace. In the process of achieving the objective of the study, several iterative steps are undertaken. First, a brief review of the literature on organizational learning and market orientation is provided. Second, a set of testable hypotheses is developed pertaining to the effects of organizational learning on market orientation. Third, the sample and measures are presented, followed by a discussion of the analysis and results. The paper concludes with the implications of the study.

ORGANIZATIONAL LEARNING AND MARKET ORIENTATION

Organizational Learning

Organizational learning is a function of two related but different concepts, including (1) the *process* of organizational learning and (2) the *structure* of the learning organization. Slater and Narver (1995, p. 63) state that, "at its most basic level, [the process of] organizational learning is the development of new knowledge or insights that have the potential to influence behavior." As such, organizational learning can be viewed as a form of innovation (Hurley and Hult, 1998). Garvin (1993, p. 80) states that the structure of the learning organization refers to "an organization skilled at creating, acquiring, and transferring knowledge, and at modifying its behavior to reflect new knowledge and insights." Slater and Narver (1994a, p. 2) argue that this type of learning "eliminates organizations that are adept at creating or acquiring new knowledge but unable to apply that knowledge to their own activities, as well as organizations whose behavior may be influenced indirectly by new knowledge." Thus, learning organizations *learn* and then *behave* accordingly. In this regard, "organizational learning is a complex, multidimensional construct occurring at different cognitive levels . . . and encompassing multiple subprocesses" (Slater and Narver, 1994, p. 2).

The process of operationalizing organizational learning is confounded by the diversity of existing paradigms proposing to define the construct (e.g., Argyris and Schön, 1978, 1996; Day, 1991, 1994; Hult, 1998; Hult and Ferrell, 1997a; Lukas, Hult, and Ferrell, 1996; Hurley and Hult, 1998; Senge,

1990; Sinkula, 1994; Slater and Narver, 1994, 1995). However, the common theme among these studies is that organizational learning is multidimensional and, therefore, made up of a set of related but distinct constructs. Using the organizational learning framework developed by Hult (1998) and Hult and Ferrell (1997a), four distinct but related "orientations" were incorporated into the study of education-related organizational learning:

1. *Team orientation:* Team orientation is defined as the degree to which educational collaboration and cooperation is present in the learning environment.
2. *Systems orientation:* Systems orientation is defined as the degree to which a "broad picture" exists of the educational elements and thus a reason certain elements exist in the learning environment.
3. *Learning orientation:* Learning orientation is defined as the degree to which the value of learning is stressed for the long-term benefits of the overall learning environment.
4. *Memory orientation:* Memory orientation is defined as the degree to which communication and distribution of knowledge is stressed in the learning environment (i.e., accessibility to knowledge).

Market Orientation

Although marketing scholars acknowledge the notion that market orientation is a key element of the marketing discipline, only recently has a systematic development of a theory of market orientation been established in two separate streams of research by Kohli and Jaworski (1990) and Narver and Slater (1990). These authors followed their conceptual works by empirically investigating the phenomenon of market orientation (Jaworski and Kohli, 1993; Slater and Narver, 1994b). Others have also followed the lead of Kohli and Jaworski's and Slater and Narver's work (e.g., Deshpande, Farley, and Webster, 1993; Ruekert, 1992; Siguaw, Brown, and Widing, 1994).

Related to the concept of organizational learning, Slater and Narver (1995) argue that Kohli and Jaworski's (1990) components of market orientation (i.e., intelligence generation, intelligence dissemination, and responsiveness) function as intermediate outcomes of organizational learning. Slater and Narver (1995) continue to suggest that their own conceptualization of market orientation (i.e., customer orientation, competitor orientation, and interfunctional coordination) function as a part of an organization's culture, which is suggested to be a determinant of organizational learning. In addition, Slater and Narver (1995) state that Jaworski and Kohli (1993) have "facilitated research on organizational learning by developing measures of the effectiveness of the information acquisition [intelligence generation], intelligence dissemination, and responsiveness stages of the learning process, which are themselves measures of intermediate outcomes" (p. 72). The three stages of intermediate outcomes of the learning process are:

1. *Intelligence generation* is defined as the collection and assessment of student needs and preferences and the forces that influence the development and refinement of those needs in a learning environment.
2. *Intelligence dissemination* is defined as the process and extent of education-related market information exchange within a learning environment.
3. *Responsiveness* is defined as the action taken in response to the intelligence that is generated and disseminated within a learning environment.

HYPOTHESIS DEVELOPMENT

The four organizational learning orientations (team orientation, systems orientation, learning orientation, and memory orientation) are hypothesized to be positively related to market orientation (intelligence generation, intelligence dissemination, and responsiveness). Each individual hypothesis is discussed and justified in the following sections.

Team orientation and market orientation. From a long-term perspective, the general principle is that an institution of higher education should be able to deliver better education and learning as a team-oriented unit (where students, faculty, and administrators are members of the team) as compared with the educational outcomes achieved by the individual members of the institutional system. However, often it seems that teams made up of highly intelligent people do not "live up to the expectations." One explanation for this is that they may have not really learned to work together (Senge, 1990). In order for an institution to function effectively as a "team," a dialogue must exist among its constituencies, where a focus exists on sharing assumptions, thinking together to solve problems, and charting future operations of the educational system. Thinking together fosters an educational system focused on creating a genuine team orientation, subsequently leading to excellence and learning because the unit's members feel that they are pursuing their own goals (Argyris and Schön, 1978; Sinkula, 1994). As such, each member of the educational system has an input in the process of creating, developing, and implementing a team orientation that leads to a commonality of direction, the harmonization of individuals' energies, and a more efficient educational system. To test this contention, the following hypotheses were examined:

H1a: Intelligence generation will be positively influenced by the team orientation existing among the students and faculty in the international marketing program.

H1b: Intelligence dissemination will be positively influenced by the team orientation existing among the students and faculty in the international marketing program.

H1c: Responsiveness will be positively influenced by the team orientation existing among the students and faculty in the international marketing program.

Systems orientation and market orientation. "Systems thinking is a discipline for seeing wholes" (Senge, 1990, p. 68). For example, individuals who can determine the outcome of a specific strategy arguably make the best problem solvers, leading to an increase in the individuals' effectiveness. Systems orientation focuses on structuring the educational elements and activities in relation to the broad "picture" and educational mission that is implemented by these educational tools. As such, systems orientation is an important dimension of learning because it helps to identify learning patterns and reinforces or changes these patterns at the organizational level (Senge, 1990; Slater and Narver, 1995). Hence, the following hypotheses were tested:

H2a: Intelligence generation will be positively influenced by the systems orientation existing among the students and faculty in the international marketing program.

H2b: Intelligence dissemination will be positively influenced by the systems orientation existing among the students and faculty in the international marketing program.

H2c: Responsiveness will be positively influenced by the systems orientation existing among the students and faculty in the international marketing program.

Learning orientation and market orientation. To foster a high degree of organizational learning, an institution has to place a high degree of value on such learning. Norman (1985, p. 231) states that "every organization learns, and every organization has a set of dominating ideas . . . they may be more or less consciously formulated and more or less visible, and they may represent good or bad interpretations of what has led to success or failure, but they are always there." Similarly, Senge (1990) talks about "mental models" as potentially inhibiting an organization's degree of learning. For example, a common problem is that many of the best educational ideas are never implemented. Often, great ideas fail to be translated into organized actions, a consequence of constraining mental models, according to Senge (1990). Developing a higher institution's capacity to work within the climate of a high degree of organizational learning requires both learning new skills and implementing a system that helps bring these skills into a regular practice (Sackmann, 1991). Thus, a university-based learning organization is a function of its consistently improved understanding of the educational system. Within this context, the following hypotheses were examined:

> H3a: Intelligence generation will be positively influenced by the learning orientation existing among the students and faculty in the international marketing program.

> H3b: Intelligence dissemination will be positively influenced by the learning orientation existing among the students and faculty in the international marketing program.

> H3c: Responsiveness will be positively influenced by the learning orientation existing among the students and faculty in the international marketing program.

Memory orientation and market orientation. The mechanisms for achieving an educational system where organizational memory is accessible when the students, faculty, and administrators need the information and in the form they want it vary (cf. Lukas, Hult, and Ferrell, 1996). For example, a tendency exists to trivialize routine learning activities because they arise so frequently (Sinkula, 1994). However, routines are a critical part of "communicating learning beyond the individual who discovers it" (Jelinik, 1979, p. 37). Related to this, Cohen (1991, p. 36) studied organizations as "processing information to learn and apply skilled routines." Once the routine is in place, a substantial barrier to information could contradict it (Sinkula, 1994), information Siegler (1983) considers the most crucial to learning. A memory orientation incorporates the notion that by performing a set of learning activities repeatedly, a shared knowledge base is developed of those activities and a means for performing better the next time. The individual member's experience leads to the modification of knowledge and subsequently to a better understanding of the educational system. To examine this proposition, the following hypotheses were tested:

> H4a: Intelligence generation will be positively influenced by the memory orientation existing among the students and faculty in the international marketing program.

> H4b: Intelligence dissemination will be positively influenced by the memory orientation existing among the students and faculty in the international marketing program.

H4c: Responsiveness will be positively influenced by the memory orientation existing among the students and faculty in the international marketing program.

METHODS

Sample

The sample used to test the research hypotheses included 193 undergraduate and graduate international marketing students at three universities in the north, midwest, and south United States. As such, the study focused on examining the emergence of organizational learning as it pertains to international marketing education, specifically where the course focus is on in-depth case study analysis (e.g., Harvard Business School cases) and comprehensive international business computer simulations (e.g., INTOPIA international business simulation). The overall sample consisted of students mostly in the 20-25 age range (n = 124), with a fairly even female/male ratio (83 females vs. 110 males), and with most of the students being from the U.S. (148 U.S. citizens vs. 45 foreign nationals).

Measurements

Table 1 provides descriptive statistics, including means, standard deviations, intercorrelations, construct reliabilities, and shared variances for the

TABLE 1. Summary Statistics for the Study Variables[a]

Variable	Mean	Std. Dev.	1	2	3	4	5	6	7
1. Team Orientation (TO)	4.49	1.08	.79	.37	.29	.29	.18	.27	.29
2. Systems Orientation (SO)	5.02	1.16	.61	.89	.34	.19	.08	.08	.21
3. Learning Orientation (LO)	5.54	.84	.54	.58	.73	.14	.16	.15	.21
4. Memory Orientation (MO)	4.57	.84	.54	.44	.38	.62	.08	.18	.14
5. Intelligence Generation (IG)	3.16	.64	.43	.29	.40	.28	.75	.42	.11
6. Intelligence Dissemination (ID)	2.93	.75	.52	.28	.39	.42	.65	.73	.16
7. Responsiveness (R)	2.94	.69	.54	.46	.46	.38	.33	.40	.85

[a]All intercorrelations are significant at the p < .01 level. Intercorrelations are included in the lower triangle of the matrix. Construct reliabilities for the study measures are underlined and included on the diagonal. Shared variances are included in the upper triangle of the matrix.

measurement scales. The items for the scales used in this study are included in the Appendix.

The psychometric properties of the scales were evaluated by confirmatory factor analysis via the use of LISREL (Jöreskog and Sörbom, 1993). The measurement models were evaluated using the DELTA2 index (Bollen, 1989) and the relative noncentrality index (RNI) (McDonald and Marsh, 1990), which have been shown to be the most stable fit indices (Gerbing and Anderson, 1992). The specific items were evaluated based on the item's error variance, modification index, and residual covariation (Anderson and Gerbing, 1988; Fornell and Larcker, 1981; Jöreskog and Sörbom, 1993).

Construct reliability was calculated using the procedures outlined by Fornell and Larcker (1981), including examining the parameter estimates and their associated t-values and assessing the average variance extracted for each construct. Discriminant validity within the multidimensional organizational learning and market orientation constructs was established by calculating the shared variance between the orientations of the construct and verifying that it was lower than the average variances extracted for the individual dimensions. Similarly, discriminant validity between the organizational learning orientations and the market orientation dimensions was also established by comparing the shared variances between the orientations of organizational learning and the market orientation dimensions and the specific subscale's average variance extracted. While the two scales are discussed in detail in the next sections, the shared variance between the four organizational learning orientations and the three market orientation dimensions range from 8% to 42% (Table 1).

Organizational learning. Organizational learning was measured by modifying the 17-item organizational learning capacity (OLC) scale developed by Hult (1998) and Hult and Ferrell (1997a) to the educational setting. The covariation among the items is explained by a correlated four-factor measurement model including the dimensions of team orientation (TO; 5 items), systems orientation (SO; 4 items), learning orientation (LO; 4 items), and memory orientation (MO; 4 items). The overall scale measures the degree of organizational learning taking place in the international marketing program and between the members of the student's major area, as defined by the activities and relationships between the student and the faculty and staff in the major area (i.e., marketing or international business). A seven-point Likert-type scale ranging from "strongly disagree" to "strongly agree" was used. DELTA2 and RNI for the four-factor solution are both .98. The parameter estimates range from .53 to .75, .72 to .97, .56 to .76, and .43 to .63 ($p < .01$) for the four dimensions of team orientation, systems orientation, learning orientation, and memory orientation, respectively. Average variances extracted and construct reliabilities are 43.4% and .79, 67.3% and .89, 40.8%

and .73, 29.7% and .62 for team orientation, systems orientation, learning orientation, and memory orientation, respectively. The shared variances among the four orientations range between 14% and 37% (Table 1).

Market orientation. Market orientation was measured by modifying the MARKOR scale developed by Kohli, Jaworski, and Kumar (1993) to the educational setting. This scale incorporates the three dimensions of intelligence generation (IG; 6 items), intelligence dissemination (ID; 5 items), and responsiveness (R; 9 items). The overall scale measures the degree of organizationwide (related to the student's major area) generation of education-related intelligence pertaining to current and future needs of students, dissemination of intelligence within the relevant part of the education system, and responsiveness to it (cf. Kohli, Jaworski, and Kumar, 1993). A five-point Likert-type scale was used ranging from "strongly disagree" to "strongly agree." DELTA2 and RNI for the three-factor solution are .93 and .94, respectively. The parameter estimates range from .42 to .71 for intelligence generation, .50 to .69 for intelligence dissemination, and .28 to .74 for responsiveness. Average variances extracted and construct reliabilities are 33.8% and .75, 35.2% and .73, and 40.3% and .85 for intelligence generation, intelligence dissemination, and responsiveness, respectively. The shared variances among the three dimensions range between 11% to 42% (Table 1).

RESULTS AND DISCUSSION

Testing of the hypothesized relationships (H1 through H4) was accomplished through the use of structural equation modeling via the use of LISREL. The results of the LISREL analysis are presented in Figure 1. DELTA2 and RNI are both .99 for the hypothesized model. The error covariance for intelligence generation and intelligence dissemination are set to free because of their close theoretical relationship (cf. Kohli and Jaworski, 1990). The specific hypotheses are discussed in the following sections.

H1. In support of H1, considerable evidence was found linking team orientation to all of the three market orientation dimensions of intelligence generation, intelligence dissemination, and responsiveness. These results are in keeping with Slater and Narver's (1995) argument that intelligence generation, intelligence dissemination, and responsiveness would serve as intermediate learning outcomes, and that organizational learning can serve as a resolution to the supply/need and equivocality problems outlined by Sinkula (1994). Thus, it would appear that team orientation not only generates information needs but generates equivocal supply as well. The results further suggest that when the sharing of experiences in a way that established a motivating team orientation is encouraged, students and faculty are more likely to generate and disseminate pertinent knowledge and to respond effec-

FIGURE 1. Structural Equation Model of Organizational Learning and Market Orientation in International Marketing Education

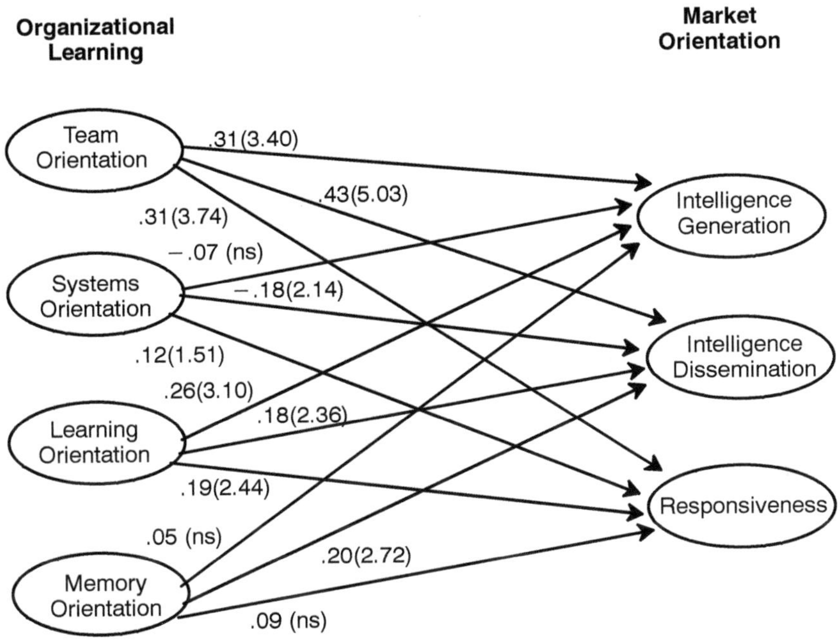

tively and appropriately to that information. This will lead to more effective and focused learning taking place in the international marketing program and the student's particular major (e.g., marketing or international business).

H2. H2 is not supported in this analysis. While systems orientation is significantly related to intelligence generation, the relationship is negative, which is contrary to the hypothesis (H2b). To stretch the implications of the results, the relationship between systems orientation and responsiveness is positive and significant at the .15 level (t-value = 1.51), while the intelligence generation and systems orientation relationship does not approach any significance level. Overall, the H2 results imply that having knowledge of the "broad picture" of the learning activities in the international marketing course and the student's particular major does not enhance the learning taking place (i.e., generation and dissemination of knowledge). In fact, systems orientation seems to hinder the dissemination of information. This result implies that if the students and faculty understand the broad mission of the international marketing program, dissemination of knowledge related to the activities and relationships in the field may inhibit the overall learning taking place.

H3. Similar to the team orientation and market orientation results, all the dimensions of market orientation (intelligence generation, intelligence dissemination, and responsiveness) are significantly and positively related to learning orientation. Thus, it appears that when the value of learning is stressed for the long-term benefits of the overall learning environment, students and faculty generate and disseminate more information and also respond to the additional knowledge in a proper and consistent manner to achieve an education-based competitive advantage.

H4. Only partial support exists for H4, linking market orientation to memory orientation. The only significant relationship was found to be the one between intelligence dissemination and memory orientation. Apparently, a memory orientation generates equivocal supply of information more so than information needs. Thus, a high degree of memory orientation helps to generate and disseminate information that is accessible when the students and faculty need it and in the form they need it. In addition, memory orientation helps to design the appropriate response to the obtained international marketing/business related information.

CONCLUSIONS

The purpose of this study was to investigate the emergence and consequent education-related outcomes of organizational learning in international marketing education. Similar to the argument by Slater and Narver (1995), the perspective taken in this paper is that both positive and normative dimensions of organizational learning are important to develop. This study should provide both, as well as suggestions for additional research that has the potential to contribute to the development of thought on organizational learning in marketing education.

The objective of education-related organizational learning should be to achieve superior learning in courses such as international marketing, subsequently providing a competitive advantage for students in their major (i.e., in this case the students represented marketing and international business majors). With the education at the university level increasingly focusing on team-based approaches to learning to stress values and behaviors valued by corporations, we need to adopt educational methods that correspond with the working environment facing our students. Market orientation, organizational learning, and innovation are not only buzzwords anymore, they are practiced by many of the most successful multinational corporations. It seems only natural that higher education takes advantage of tools that have proven successful in making business operations more efficient and effective, leading to a sustainable competitive advantage instead of a simple short-term oriented competitive advantage.

An integrated marketing coursework designed around the four organizational learning orientations should lead to students achieving a competitive advantage vis-a-vis their counterparts in the marketplace. As such, the function of the organizational learning framework in structuring marketing education means that education-related people (i.e., administrators, faculty, and students) put aside their old ways of thinking about details (learning orientation), adopt a broader perspective of how the marketplace really works in relation to the education offered (systems orientation), learn to be open with each other (memory orientation), and work together to form and implement a marketing education strategy upon which everyone can agree (team orientation) (Hult and Ferrell, 1997a, 1997b).

The results of this study also support the prevailing trend in restructuring organizational units to reflect organizational learning capacity (e.g., Day, 1991, 1994; Hult, 1998; Hult and Ferrell, 1997a; Hult and Ferrell, 1997b; Hurley and Hult, 1998; Lukas, Hult, and Ferrell, 1996; Senge, 1990; Sinkula, 1994; Slater and Narver, 1995). The study provides empirical support for emerging conceptual frameworks that the *process* of organizational learning and the *structure* of the learning organization can contribute to increased competitive advantage and improved performance in university programs, a unique and valued contribution in that successful business practices can be brought into the classroom. While the inferences are restrictive (due to the fine-grained nature of the study), they extend the evidence of the benefits of organizational learning beyond the theoretical stage, and point toward possible relationships with other performance indicants (e.g., student satisfaction, commitment to the university).

REFERENCES

Anderson, James C. and Gerbing, David W. (1988). Some Methods for Respecifying Measurement Models to Obtain Unidimensional Construct Measurement. *Journal of Marketing Research* 19 (November): 453-460.

Argyris, Chris and Schön, Donald A. (1978). *Organizational Learning: A Theory of Action Perspective*. Reading, MA: Addison-Wesley Publishing Company.

Argyris, Chris and Schön, Donald A. (1996). *Organizational Learning II: Theory, Method, and Practice.* Reading, MA: Addison-Wesley Publishing Company.

Bollen, Kenneth A., (1989). *Structural Equations with Latent Variables*. New York, NY: Wiley & Sons.

Cohen, Michael D. (1991). Individual Learning and Organizational Routine: Emerging Connections. *Organization Science*, 2 (February): 135-139.

Day, George S. (1991). Learning about Markets. *Marketing Science Institute Report Number 91-117*. Cambridge, MA: Marketing Science Institute.

Day, George S. (1994). The Capabilities of Market-Driven Organizations. *Journal of Marketing* 58: 37-52.

Deshpande, Rohit, Farley, John U., and Webster, Frederick E. (1993). Corporate Culture, Customer Orientation, and Innovativeness in Japanese Firms. *Journal of Marketing* 57 (January): 23-27.

Dumaine, Brian. (1994). Mr. Learning Organization. *Fortune* (October 17): 147-157.

Fornell, Claes and Larcker, David F. (1991). Evaluating Structural Equation Models with Unobservable Variables and Measurement Error. *Journal of Marketing Research* 18 (February): 39-50.

Garvin, David A. (1993). Building a Learning Organization. *Harvard Business Review* 71: 78-91.

Gerbing, David W. and Anderson, James C. (1992). Monte Carlo Evaluations of Goodness of Fit Indices for Structural Equation Models. *Sociological Methods and Research* 21, 132-160.

Hult, G. Tomas M. (1998). Managing the International Strategic Sourcing Process as a Market-Driven Organizational Learning System. *Decision Sciences*, 29(1), 193-216.

Hult, G. Tomas M. and Ferrell, O.C. (1997a). Global Organizational Learning Capacity in Purchasing: Construct and Measurement. *Journal of Business Research*, 40(2), 97-113.

Hult, G. Tomas M. and Ferrell, O.C. (1997b). A Global Learning Organization Structure and Market Information Processing. *Journal of Business Research*, 40(2), 155-167.

Hurley, Robert F. and G. Tomas M. Hult. (1998). Innovation, Market Orientation, and Organizational Learning: An Integration and Empirical Examination. *Journal of Marketing* 62(3), 42-54.

Jaworski, Bernard J. and Kohli, Ajay K. (1993). Market orientation: Antecedents and Consequences. *Journal of Marketing* 57 (July): 53-70.

Jelinik, Mariann (1979). *Institutionalizing Innovation: A Study of Organizational Learning Systems*. New York, NY: Praeger Publishers.

Jöreskog, Karl G. and Sörbom, Dag. (1993). *LISREL 8: A Guide to the Program and Applications*. Chicago, IL: SPSS.

Kohli, Ajay K. and Jaworski, Bernard J. (1990). Market Orientation: The Construct, Research Propositions, and Managerial Implications. *Journal of Marketing* 54 (April): 1-8.

Kohli, Ajay K., Jaworski, Bernard J., Kumar, Ajith. (1993). MARKOR: A Measure of Market Orientation. *Journal of Marketing Research* 15 (November): 467-477.

Lukas, Bryan A., Hult, G. Tomas M., and Ferrell, O.C. (1996). A Theoretical Perspective of the Antecedents and Consequences of Organizational Learning in Marketing Channels. *Journal of Business Research* 36: 233-244.

McDonald, Roderick P. and Marsh, Herbert W. (1990). Choosing a Multivariate Model: Noncentrality and Goodness of Fit. *Psychological Bulletin* 107: 247-255.

Narver, John C. and Slater, Stanley F. (1990). The Effect of Market Orientation on Business Profitability. *Journal of Marketing* 54 (October): 20-35.

Norman, Richard. (1985). Developing Capabilities for Organizational Learning,. In *Organizational Strategy and Change*, Johannes M. Pennings, Ed. San Francisco, CA: Jossey-Bass.

Ruekert, Robert W. (1992). Developing a Market Orientation: An Organizational Strategy Perspective. *International Journal of Research in Marketing* 9 (September): 225-245.

Sackmann, Sonja A. (1991). *Cultural Knowledge in Organizations*. Newbury Park, CA: Sage Publications.

Senge, Peter M. (1993). *The Fifth Discipline: The Art and Practice of the Learning Organization*. New York, NY: Doubleday/ Currency.

Siegler, R.S. (1983). Five Generalizations about Cognitive Development. *American Psychologist* 38 (March): 263-277.

Siguaw, Judy A., Brown, Gene, and Widing, Robert E., II, (1993). The Influence of the Market Orientation of the Firm on Sales Force behavior and Attitudes. *Journal of Marketing* 31 (February): 106-116.

Sinkula, James M. (1994). Market Information Processing and Organizational Learning. *Journal of Marketing* 58 (January): 35-45.

Slater, Stanley F. and Narver, John C. (1994a). Market Oriented Isn't Enough: Build a Learning Organization. *Marketing Science Institute Report Number 94-103*. Cambridge, MA: Marketing Science Institute.

Slater, Stanley F. and Narver, John C. (1994b). Does Competitive Environment Moderate the Market Orientation–Performance Relationship? *Journal of Marketing* 58 (January): 46-55.

Slater, Stanley F. and Narver, John C. (1995). Market Orientation and the Learning Organization. *Journal of Marketing*, 59: 63-74.

APPENDIX

Measure Scales

Scale	Items
Team Orientation	• A team spirit among the students and the teachers is common. • Around here, teamwork is the common way of working rather than an exception to the norm. • There is a commonality of purpose in my major field of study. • There is total agreement on the educational vision among the school's professors, administrators, and students. • Our teachers are committed to sharing their vision for the educational process with us.
Systems Orientation	• We have a good sense of how the courses tie together in our major to give us a good education. • We understand the value of the courses we take as a part of our major and how each of them fits into the major. • All the activities that take place in our classes are clearly defined. • We understand where all activities fit in in our course work.
Learning Orientation	• The basic values of our education include learning as a key to improvement. • The collective wisdom at this school is one that encourages learning. • The general feeling among professors, administrators, and students is that learning is an investment not an expense. • Learning in our major field of study is seen as a commodity.
Memory Orientation	• We have a specific method for sharing lessons learned in our courses. • We always audit unsuccessful learning behaviors and communicate what we learned to our fellow students. • People at our school often talk to each other about past educational experiences. • Our school has formal routines to uncover "bad" teaching.
Intelligence Generation	• We meet with our teachers frequently to discuss our educational goals. • We do a lot of research to improve our learning.

APPENDIX (continued)

Measure Scales

Scale	Items
Intelligence Generation	• We are fast at detecting changes in our educational preferences. • We contact our teacher in our major field of study frequently to assess the quality of our work. • We are fast at detecting fundamental changes in our educational environment. • We periodically review the likely effect of changes in the educational environment on our overall education.
Intelligence Dissemination	• Students frequently have meetings to discuss trends and developments at our school and in our major. • We spend time discussing future educational needs with our teacher. • When something happens in a class–any class in our major–we know about it in a short period of time. • Information on student satisfaction at our school is given to all people involved in providing us on a regular basis. • When we find out something important about the educational system, we tell our fellow students as soon as possible.
Responsiveness	• Our school responds fast when universities around here change their tuition. • Our school is receptive to changes in students' educational needs. • Our school periodically reviews the curriculum to ensure that they are in line with what the students want. • Students, administrators, and faculty get together periodically to plan a response to changes taking place in our educational environment. • If a university in our area were to launch an intensive campaign targeted at this university's current and potential students, our school would implement a response immediately. • The activities of the different departments at our school are well coordinated. • Student complaints are taken seriously at our school. • If our school came up with a great marketing plan, it probably would be able to implement it in a timely fashion. • When our school finds out that the students would like to modify a course, schedule, or any part of their education, it makes a concerted effort to do so.

Learning from Students' Perceptions of International Business

Alma Mintu-Wimsatt

SUMMARY. The debate continues on the internationalization of the business curricula. However, little attention has been given on how undergraduate students actually feel about international business. While students should not be the source for prescriptives on how to teach a course, their views on certain issues can help provide the framework for the development and integration of international business in existing courses and/or the current business curricula. This paper discusses issues pertaining to undergraduate business students' perceptions on international business. Students from a non-urban regional state university, which currently does not offer a degree or certification program in international business, are utilized in this study. *[Article copies available for a fee from The Haworth Document Delivery Service: 1-800-342-9678. E-mail address: getinfo@haworthpressinc.com <Website: http://www.haworthpressinc.com>]*

INTRODUCTION

Business programs across the United States are continuously striving to enhance and broaden students' exposure to the realities of the international

---

Alma Mintu-Wimsatt is Associate Professor of Marketing, Department of Marketing & Management, Texas A & M University-Commerce, Commerce, TX 75429 (E-mail: alma_wimsatt@TAMU-commerce.edu).

The author would like to thank Drs. Keith McFarland and Lee Schmidt for their support. The author would also like to thank the members of the IB Task Force, the Editor and the reviewers for their comments.

This study was funded by the Graduate School and the College of Business & Technology at TAMU-Commerce.

[Haworth co-indexing entry note]: "Learning from Students' Perceptions of International Business." Mintu-Wimsatt, Alma. Co-published simultaneously in *Journal of Teaching in International Business* (The International Business Press, an imprint of The Haworth Press, Inc.) Vol. 10, No. 3/4, 1999, pp. 99-112; and: *Teaching and Program Variations in International Business* (ed: Erdener Kaynak and John R. Schermerhorn, Jr.) The International Business Press, an imprint of The Haworth Press, Inc., 1999, pp. 99-112. Single or multiple copies of this article are available for a fee from The Haworth Document Delivery Service [1-800-342-9678, 9:00 a.m. - 5:00 p.m. (EST). E-mail address: getinfo@haworthpressinc.com].

business arena. Now, more than ever, business academicians and practitioners have witnessed the interconnected web of the world economy that necessitates the need for the international orientation. The international orientation is also further reinforced by the American Assembly of Collegiate Schools of Business' (AACSB) new accreditation standards that call for, among others, coverage of global issues as one of the key dimensions of business education. The rationale for this emphasis stems from the need for students to be informed, competitive, and knowledgeable about the global business environment. As far as business students are concerned, the global environment is most likely to influence their prospective work environments as well as career paths several years after graduation.

Trends relating to the globalization of the business curricula have led many universities to offer various programs ranging from international business-related classes (e.g., International Marketing, Global Distribution) to Bachelor degrees in international business (Gwin, 1995). Typically, the international business programs are initiated by the various functional departments and/or mandated by the administration. Hence, the unidirectional "top-down" approach is implemented, with students following the requirements and having minimal input or feedback on the various programs. The top-down approach is valid and perpetuated since the drivers for change are often the experts with significant experience and knowledge in international business.

To gauge the effectiveness of any international business program, the participants of the programs also need to be considered. Unfortunately, little is known about students' actual perceptions of international business. Students' perceptions can be important to the development of the business curricula since there are several elements to "teaching" and "learning" about international business (i.e., "bottom-up" approach). For example, an undergraduate from a regional state university may or may not have the same in-depth appreciation for international business as a student enrolled in a more cosmopolitan private institution.

Regardless of the use of the top-down or bottom-up approach, ultimately, academicians need to understand their students as well as corporate clientele before leaping into the complicated task of internationalizing any part of the curricula. Exploring students' perceptions can provide the business school with a means to evaluate the current curricula and pinpoint where changes ought to be made. These perceptions can then be related to corporate practices–connecting what businesses want and what students must learn. Perhaps, in examining the primary stakeholders of higher education, the business school and its faculty members can be provided with directives on where to start, who should be involved, and to what extent should changes be made. These directives are important in light of the common budgetary constraints, lack of faculty training, and absence of other support methods necessary to truly offer a *legitimate* international program.

Towards achieving this goal, this study is unique since it takes a "bottom-up" approach to IB. In particular, this paper presents a descriptive study that examines business students' perceptions on how their current programs are preparing them for international business. It also looks at students' anticipated role in international business upon completion of their [business] degrees. By assessing students' views on issues relating to international business, appropriate actions for internationalizing the curricula can be recommended [within the parameters of our university].

LITERATURE REVIEW

Globalization of the Business Curricula

Several studies have looked at the importance of the international business (hereafter IB) perspective (cf., Cavusgil, 1993) in business education. It is anticipated that IB will continue to be a major concern in education given the information technology growth, the regionalization of economic activities, the interdependence of global economies, the preoccupation towards the "global consumer," and the popularity of strategic alliances worldwide, among others (Turley et al., 1993). To meet these trends, business education has responded by offering a range of initiatives and programs that are responsive to the changes in the way business is being conducted.

As a result, a dearth of information has been provided on topical areas such as: strategic approaches to IB education; IB faculty training; required administrative support; and, curriculum development (Andrus et al., 1995). Without any doubt, the research on the area has provided an avenue for universities and colleges to re-evaluate their existing programs. Several prescriptives and/or agenda have also been suggested to help create, if not enhance, the teaching approach to IB (Andrus et al., 1995).

Bottom-Up Approach

Students' Perceptions. Despite much progress in the area, however, business students' perceptions on IB are often undermined. Note, however, that it is not this author's intent to suggest that these students should be the primary drivers for any curriculum changes. Indeed, students' perception may be limited for the obvious reason that they do not have a working knowledge of the field. But, their views on certain issues can help provide the framework for the development and integration of international business in existing courses and/or the current business curricula. These perceptions, as a form of feedback information, can be compared with what corporations are actually doing and what prospective employees ought to be familiar with as part of their academic training.

Consider the following scenario:

> University XYZ is a regional state university located about 80 miles from a large metropolitan area. The student data profile indicates that most of its business undergraduates commute from neighboring rural towns, come from families whereby they may be among the few to receive a college education, and desire to reside in small towns after graduation.

Presented above is a situation whereby a proponent of IB cannot simply mandate an overhaul of the business curricula and offer courses, degrees, certification, or study abroad programs immediately. It would even be presumptuous to think that the above students would see any value to IB. Indeed, for some of these students, IB may be perceived as being irrelevant and a barrier towards early graduation.

If this is true, it may be necessary to first examine the target audience as well as re-evaluate current course offerings. Building interest, and hopefully, a parallel demand for IB [by encouraging students to think "beyond the box"] are critical to the success and effectiveness of IB in any business school.

With this type of student mindset, the task of setting forth an IB agenda can be quite complicated, if not challenging. Some universities can offer degrees or certificates in IB, form alliances with foreign universities, provide internships with multinational corporations, and offer short-term study abroad programs immediately. On the other hand, a non-urban regional state university such as ours is preoccupied with budget cuts, freezing/lack of faculty lines, and other administrative issues. Despite these obstacles, business faculty members at our university realize that we will be doing our students disservice if we do not develop a well-rounded business academic background which includes some emphasis on the IB component.

Where Do Businesses Fit? Likewise, business schools need to look at what prospective employers think of their programs, particularly IB. For example, is IB important to prospective employers? Is there a prevailing interest in hiring IB graduates? Or, do employers prefer to hire students with a business degree coupled with IB-related classes?

The preliminary analysis of a recent survey of corporate employers[1] located in one of the major cities of the United States indicates that a majority [of these employers] regard the international orientation and global thinking as critical in today's business environment. However, despite its importance, corporations do not readily assign newly hired undergraduates to international business activities. Instead, new employees are first expected to familiarize themselves with the dynamics of the organization and receive additional in-house training. It may be approximately 1-2 years before these employees are actually exposed to international business. But, these employers admit that academic training and/or interest in IB areas such as exporting, international business law, and exchange rates facilitate the process of being placed in IB positions.

The Dilemma

Herein lies the dilemma for those in academia. While corporations [who presumably will be employing our college graduates] value IB education, some business students perceive its importance differently. While the hypothetical student situation presented earlier may not be familiar to many, it does exist. Indeed, it has oftentimes presented this author with the challenge of how to get students to be more cognizant of the importance of IB.

At a small, non-urban regional state university such as ours, students are not only constrained by their own financial resources, but many fail to recognize the relevance of IB in their immediate environment. In fact, a large number of our students have not even traveled around the United States to experience and/or witness the implications of IB. Where the WalMart case story may be interesting and familiar to our student body, the implications of the merger between Daimler and Chrysler is of little interest to them. After all, if they do not intend nor do they envision buying a Chrysler or a Mercedes, why bother learning about the merger?

Given the practical limitations prevalent among regional state universities as well as the necessity for developing a strong IB presence within the business college, an IB task force [which included this author] decided that the first course of action ought to include the evaluation of students' perceptions of IB. The task force rationalized that perhaps, the findings will provide us with some insights on how to enhance the international orientation among business students.

More importantly, it was viewed that the students' feedback can then provide the business school with the springboard for evaluating the curricula

---

1. To date, the survey on corporate employers has not been completely analyzed. This survey focused on hiring practices as well as IB topic areas perceived by corporate employers to have the most value.

and the academic training needs of prospective employers. The rationale here stems from the fact that if indeed business students [as the task force suspected] attach little importance to IB while corporations put a premium on IB academic training, corrective curricula-related actions ought to be taken. After all, we educate students in their respective fields of specialization with the hope that at the end of the learning process, new and challenging opportunities are afforded to them.

METHODOLOGY

The primary focus of this researcher was to examine IB perceptions among business undergraduate students as a means to evaluate the perceived relevance of IB. Ultimately, the goals for undertaking this two-part project are to compare these perceptions with the current needs to corporate employers and to present viable recommendations to the Administration.

Sample

Students' perceptions regarding IB were determined using a self-administered questionnaire. The 20-item questionnaire was developed and previously utilized by one of the flagship institutions of the state as a means to enhance international education opportunities. The items ranged from Likert-type scales to open-ended questions. Senior-level marketing research students were required to solicit respondents from each of the four undergraduate levels through a quota system. As such, students from each level were well represented, no duplication (i.e., students completing 2 surveys) occurred, and respondents did not feel intimidated to respond according to their true evaluation of the situation in our university.

A total of 113 undergraduate business students from a regional state university located 80 miles from a large metropolitan area completed the survey. Out of the 113 students sampled, there were 23 freshmen, 27 sophomores, 28 juniors, and 35 seniors; and most (65%) had not traveled outside the United States. Table 1 reports the respondent profile.

Currently, these undergraduate business students are offered a limited array of IB-related courses and the business school does not offer a degree or certificate program on IB. In addition, study abroad opportunities are available every summer to countries such as Mexico, England and Jamaica. The business school is accredited by AACSB, and therefore, serious efforts have been made to integrate the global component into most of the classes, particularly the core courses.

TABLE 1. Respondent Profile

Level	Responses	Travel Abroad? YES	Travel Abroad? NO
Freshman	23	3	20
Sophomore	27	11	15
Junior	28	10	18
Senior	35	15	20
TOTAL	113	39	73

RESULTS

As can be noted in Table 1, most of the business students represented in this sample have not traveled abroad. However, it is noted that upper division students (i.e., seniors and juniors) were more likely to have traveled abroad than their lower division counterparts (i.e., freshmen and sophomores). It is important that the question regarding travel abroad is emphasized since several research studies have shown that this variable is highly related to students' international orientation (Gordon and Smith, 1992).

It is alarming to note that 43.7 percent of the sample were **tentative** (i.e., "I do not know" and "probably" responses) in their opinions regarding the extent to which the education they are currently receiving at the university is preparing them to interact with people from other countries and/or cultures (Table 2). Worst, a third of the respondents think they are not being prepared at all (i.e., "No" response).

To further elaborate on the above question, we also asked students what factors attributed to their inability to avail themselves of programs [such as study abroad opportunities, academic courses] that could enhance their IB orientation. Forty-three percent (43%) stated that cost was the primary limiting factor while twenty-three percent (23%) indicated time as the reason. As for their perceptions regarding enrolling in foreign language courses and its implications on the international orientation, thirty-two percent (32%) indicated that taking a language class enhanced their business communication skills while twenty-eight percent (28%) claimed it enhanced their basic communication skills. Thirteen percent indicated that they were not interested in any language courses (13%).

The respondents were also asked a general question relating to the importance of the global perspective in their education. The participants believed that developing a global perspective in their field of study had "some level of importance" (see Table 3). Although the freshmen sample reported the lowest level of perceived importance, this is not surprising considering the limited number of classes they have taken in the university. The level of perceived importance seems to slightly improve as they move on to the higher levels. However, none of these mean values were significantly different from each other at the .05 level.

Four specific IB-related questions were also asked of the participants. The mean values presented in Table 4 suggest that, in general, the business undergraduate sample in this study were not inclined to associate traveling abroad as part of their future career requirements. As such, it is not surprising that they are not enthusiastic about living abroad as part of their career paths. Likewise, they do not think that they will have to deal with managers, bosses, and customers from other countries. These findings tend to reinforce the student profile of the university's undergraduate students.

TABLE 2. How Prepared Are Students?

Do you believe the classes you have taken or will take at University XYZ prepare you to interact with people from other countries/cultures?	Freshman	Sophomore	Junior	Senior	TOTAL
Yes	4	7	6	7	24
No	7	4	11	12	34
Probably	4	9	9	9	31
I do not know	5	5	1	3	14
TOTAL	20	25	27	31	103

TABLE 3. Responses to Global-Related Questions (1 = Extremely Important; 2 = Very Important; 3 = Somewhat Important; 4 = Not Important)

Questions	Freshman	Sophomore	Junior	Senior	TOTAL
In your opinion, how important is it to take courses to develop a global perspective in your field of study?	2.5	2.38	2.07	2.21	2.27

TABLE 4. Responses to Global-Related Questions (1 = Extremely Likely; 2 = Very Likely; 3 = Somewhat Likely; 4 = Not Likely)

Questions	Fresh-man	Sopho-more	Junior	Senior	TOTAL
In thinking of your future, how likely is it that your career will require you to **travel abroad?**	2.56	3.26	2.86	2.86	2.86
In thinking about your future, how likely is it that your career will require you to **live abroad?**	3.09	3.81	3.46	3.47	3.71
In thinking about your future, how likely is it that your career will require you to **deal with managers and customers from other countries?**	2.22	3.01	2.53	2.47	2.56
In thinking about your future, how likely is it that your **supervisor or employer will be from another country?**	2.72	3.19	3.17	2.97	3.04

WHAT THE FINDINGS MEAN?

Without any doubt, the findings in the preceding section are quite insightful. In general, this sample finds *some* importance in taking courses to enrich their global perspective, despite the fact that they do not anticipate that their future careers will be highly affected by IB. The global perspective appears to be more important to upper division business students.

The perceived importance of IB is a critical finding, since it appears that for many of these students, the learning experience in the classroom will be their primary means of gaining exposure in the area. Many have not traveled outside the U.S. nor do they anticipate being highly involved in IB upon graduation. While foreign language and other IB-related courses are perceived to enhance business communication skills, they are time consuming. For students not predisposed toward IB, factors relating to costs and time are cited as primary reasons for the lack of enthusiasm in [IB] programs. Evidently, traveling abroad [and therefore gaining more exposure] is not a high priority.

Perhaps, the most disappointing finding relates to students' perceptions on the quality of their education. In particular, approximately a third of the sample feel that their current educational training is not preparing them to interact with people from other cultures. Regardless of whether students anticipate having to deal with foreigners in the future, they still find that this preparation component is not effectively accomplished in their classes.

WHERE DO WE START?

To help students prepare themselves in the competitive workplace, increasing their awareness as well as understanding of the various elements of global business are necessary. As a result, many business schools have responded by internationalizing their programs. Evidence of this trend is presented by Arpan et al.'s (1993) extensive study on international business education.

However, an anomaly is presented in this study whereby undergraduate business students from a non-urban regional state university are not quite cognizant nor concerned with the importance of IB. Indeed, the findings in this study present an interesting challenge to any business school. *How do we enlighten students with minimal interest and perhaps, even minimal perceived value, in IB? Where do we start?*

Outlined below are some suggestions toward answering the above questions. Note that given the type of undergraduate students enrolled in our university, recommendations for short-term study abroad programs are not included. While the impact of going abroad on students' mindset cannot be undermined, the financial resources of our students is also a key point to be considered.

Next Step: Look at Corporations

Now that we have explored students' perceptions, the next step ought to include the examination of businesses' employment requirements and their impressions of IB programs. A comparison can be made between these two constituencies which can help serve as a springboard on which courses ought to be changed or added. If students wonder why certain courses are required/changed in their degree plans, professors can always pragmatically respond by citing employer needs as driving forces for the change. I suspect that if future employment is at stake, students [and even administrators and legislators] would be more interested, if not amenable, to changes in the curricula.

Bench Marking

Armed with the findings generated from this study, another efficient means for enhancing IB education would be to look at other universities with similar experiences. For example, information can be sought from *"sister"* schools regarding some of their courses of action on internationalizing the business curricula. Sister schools are often made-up with students with similar student profiles and are faced with similar constraints. One university's mistakes as well as successes can serve as learning tools for another. Moreover, the university [and the school of business] can also bench mark against other international business programs across the country and examine both public and private universities, large and small. Not all programs require study abroad programs or have foreign language requirements and yet, they are still successful.

Find an Advocate

At a recent conference of the Southwest Academy of International Business (March, 1998), a panel of practitioners and academicians discussed the issue on how to get started in internationalizing the business curricula. The consensus response pointed towards finding key decision-makers (i.e., administration) to "buy" into the idea. If these decision-makers are committed towards the goal of internationalization, their support for new program initiatives, new faculty lines, research grants, release time to those developing new courses, and hopefully, additional funding can be forthcoming. Their support can help facilitate the internationalization process.

Create Awareness Among Students

The findings in this study clearly show that the IB mindset and experiences of lower and upper-division college students are significantly different. This is an important consideration since most college students begin taking business courses during their junior year. Therefore, their exposure to global thinking will always be an issue during their early years in college.

Perhaps, critical to the situation in our university is for students, regardless of their major, to recognize the importance of the international orientation. Moreover, it is imperative that business students recognize why IB is important. As an accredited university, this has been somewhat accomplished through the new AACSB standards focusing on the global component. Nonetheless, core classes ought to spend some time dwelling on the IB issue throughout the semester rather than simply leaving it towards the end of the term when it is often discussed haphazardly. Also, workshops, guest speakers and other audio visual presentations can help facilitate the process. The key is to provide students with avenues for exposure that can help develop their interest for IB, which in turn, facilitates the learning process.

Assess Current Course Offerings

Given the prevailing budgetary constraints of many colleges including ours, it would be unreasonable to seek funding for an entirely new IB department. Regardless of Administrative support received, creating a new department is not only tedious and time-consuming, but also politically risky at a university-wide setting.

A more pragmatic approach would be to look at the current course offerings and find out where more emphasis on IB can be integrated. This aspect of curriculum development is critical in our situation since we have to start with the challenge of inculcating in students' minds the merits of IB. Above anything else, the foundation for IB's importance to their educational experience has to be clearly presented.

Therefore, start with what the business school is currently offering, particularly the core classes. For example, in the Monetary Economics course, the role of the International Monetary Fund (IMF) should be emphasized both at the theoretical and practical levels. Given the current Asian financial fiasco–this topic should be quite timely. In International Finance classes, the role of exchange rate policies in the problems of Mexico and Asia can be underscored. Likewise, motivation theories in Management classes can help explain the work ethic of different cultures. In Accounting, the cost interpretation of bribery ought to engage students in a lively discussion while Marketing Management can dwell on the cultural environment and its impact on the creation of goods and services. Herein are examples of conscious efforts to integrate the global perspective into the current course offerings.

For some courses, the situation may be different. International Marketing, for example, has been found to be one of the key classes where the elements of international business can be extensively studied (cf., Arpan et al., 1993). Indeed, Andrus et al. (1995) have found that this course has been utilized as the focal point in the efforts toward internationalizing the business curricula. International Marketing has become the "natural" choice since most of the issues relevant to international managers (i.e., cultural environment, pricing, strategic planning) are all part of the course. However, Andrus et al. (1995) also noted that a separate International Marketing class is not necessary *if* the business curriculum has truly integrated the international component.

Faculty Involvement

Many faculty members are not inclined to participate in the internationalization efforts of the curriculum since support to strengthen and develop teaching and research is, at best, minimal (cf., Arpan et al., 1993). Given this reality, it is imperative that "appropriate" faculty members are chosen.

Ideally, faculty members with experience in the area–through consulting work, personal travel, or research–should be tapped first. This is necessary since business students need to be exposed to professors who have expertise in the area. Otherwise, instructors' credibility as well as effectiveness in the classroom can be seriously jeopardized.

However, in situations where a college has a small number of faculty members, the individual who is genuinely interested to undertake the internationalization endeavor ought to be considered. Preparing to teach an IB-related class can be time-consuming, especially if one is teaching the course for the first time. The whole scheme of teaching business dramatically changes especially when the elements of culture, international law and work ethics are factored into the learning experience. Hence, a faculty member has much work ahead of him/her in teaching this class. Fortunately, several excellent textbooks have been developed coupled with supplemental materials that can help the prospective instructor. Likewise, several Centers for International Business and Research have made available research grants, continuing education, and other current materials to aid IB instructors.

Departmental Support

If internationalization of the curriculum is to occur, this has to be reflected in the way departmental resources are allocated. First and foremost, Andrus et al. (1995) contend that tenure and promotion decisions have to reinforce the commitment for internationalizing the curricula. A faculty member's efforts toward as well as contributions to the internationalization activities of the business college have to be regarded with value. Otherwise, no one is going to seriously undertake the project.

Faculty members may also need student assistants to help develop/improve their teaching materials, gather more information, and develop case studies. To remain current in the field and maintain a network with other IB academic colleagues, some will have to attend conferences and seminars on a regular basis. Others will require more funding to legitimately establish a research stream in the field–a complex and difficult area of study (cf., Caves, 1998).

CONCLUSIONS

Presented above are pragmatic recommendations on how to enhance international business, given the prevailing mindset of our business students.

Indeed, there are many challenges ahead. Given the unique situation presented here, the drivers for change may have to come from among the faculty members whose target audience may not necessarily perceive any immediate value to their internationalization effort. The absence of resources ought not to deter academicians in providing students with an international orientation. But, in the true meaning of providing students with life-long learning experiences, academicians have to forge ahead.

REFERENCES

Andrus, David, Jay Launghlin and Wayne Norvell. (1995). "Internationalizing the Marketing Curriculum: A Profile of the International Marketing Course." *Marketing Education Review*, 5(2), 9-18.

Arpan, J., W. Folks and C. Kwok. (1993). "International Business Education in the 1990s: A Global Survey." *The American Assembly of Collegiate Schools of Business*, St Louis, MO.

Caves, Richard. (1998). "Research on International Business: Problems and Prospects." *Journal of International Business Studies*, 29(1), 5-19.

Cavusgil, S.T. (1993). "Internationalizing of Business Education: Defining the Challenge," in *Internationalizing the Business Education–Meeting the Challenge.* S.T. Cavusgil (ed)., East Lansing, MI.

Gordon, Peter. (1992). "Planning, Organizing, and Executing Short-Term International Exposures for U.S. Students of Marketing and Business." *Marketing Education Review*, 2(1), 47-54.

Gwin, John. (1995). "The International Experience Choice: A Decision Model Approach." *Marketing Education Review*, 5(2), 45-56.

SWFAD Academy of International Business session on "State of International Business: Past, Present, Future," Dallas, TX.

Turley, L., Richard Shannon, and Mark Miller. (1993). "International Marketing: Student Attitudes and Behavior." *Marketing Education Review*, 3 (Spring), 52-57.

Information System Development in a Global Environment

Kenneth R. Gray

SUMMARY. In this article the basic components of an information system in a multinational context are reviewed. Based upon these components, three types of generic challenges in developing a multinational information system are suggested: (1) managing the planning and development of the system; (2) challenges of data collection; and (3) technological and legal challenges related to transborder data flows. Finally, a local approach to information system development is outlined as the response corporations must take to achieve and maintain global competitiveness. *[Article copies available for a fee from The Haworth Document Delivery Service: 1-800-342-9678. E-mail address: getinfo@haworthpressinc.com <Website: http://www.haworthpressinc.com>]*

INTRODUCTION

Goods and services must compete today in the international marketplace with the power centers of North America, Asia, the European Union, and soon, the newly free Eastern European states. Managers are faced with the fact that they must expand and compete in overseas markets to realize sustained market share and to reap the benefits of continued business growth.

Kenneth R. Gray is Senior Fulbright Scholar, AL Akhawayn Univeristy, and Associate Professor of International Management, School of Business & Industry, Florida A & M University, One S.B.I. Plaza, Tallahassee, FL 32307-5200 (grayk40@hotmailcom).

[Haworth co-indexing entry note]: "Information System Development In a Global Environment." Gray, Kenneth R. Co-published simultaneously in *Journal of Teaching in International Business* (The International Business Press, an imprint of The Haworth Press, Inc.) Vol. 10, No. 3/4, 1999, pp. 113-128; and: *Teaching and Program Variations in International Business* (ed: Erdener Kaynak and John R. Schermerhorn, Jr.) The International Business Press, an imprint of The Haworth Press, Inc., 1999, pp. 113-128. Single or multiple copies of this article are available for a fee from The Haworth Document Delivery Service [1-800-342-9678, 9:00 a.m. - 5:00 p.m. (EST). E-mail address: getinfo@haworthpressinc.com].

Expansion means creation of mergers or strategic cooperative partnerships with firms abroad, such as the recent Chrysler/Mercedes merger, the General Motors and Toyota joint venture on Geo automobiles or the partnership of IBM and Siemens to develop high-capacity memory chips to combat Fujitsu in the European computer market (Czinkota, Ronkainen, and Tarrant, 1995). The globalization of business means the creation of a physical presence overseas to put products and services closer to their intended markets. Examples in North America include the BMW's automotive plant in South Carolina and the Daimler Benz operation in Alabama.

Of particular importance in this global push is a domestic organization's information systems. Manufacturing organizations must be able to manage and organize operations in different countries, with different currencies, suppliers, and labor rules. Financial organizations have already recognized that, with the use of advanced information and telecommunications technology, markets are essentially open 24 hours a day (Bryan & Farrell, 1996). To remain competitive, they must trade in monetary markets in London, New York, and Tokyo at any one time of a business day. In today's global marketplace, consumer goods must be as viable in Far Eastern and Middle Eastern markets as they are in a domestic market (Ohmae, 1995). The backbone of all these global endeavors will be the business's information systems which store, manipulate, and disseminate the data generated by daily business activity.

Compared with the goods and services they sell, managers are discovering that information systems are not as general and transportable across national borders. An information system of a multinational business organization is vastly more varied and complex than one of its domestic operations. Multinational information systems must have the capacity to cross multiple time zones, governments, languages, and currencies. What is of primary concern is how to develop high-quality information systems quickly enough to support organizational decision makers as they operate in this expanded environment. Doz and Prahalad (1984) assert "Coordination is the key to competitive advantage." Information systems can provide that coordination, but they must be developed fast enough to provide strategic support that the competition cannot easily or cheaply match. Therefore, a systematic approach is needed for the development of a global information system and for anticipating the special problems that may be presented in a multinational context. This article reviews the basic components of an information system in a multinational context. Based upon these components, three types of generic challenges in developing a multinational information system are suggested: (1) managing the planning and development of the system; (2) challenges of data collection; and (3) technological and legal challenges related to transborder data flows. Finally, a local approach to information system development is outlined as the response corporations must take to achieve and maintain global competitiveness.

BASIC COMPONENTS OF GLOBAL INFORMATION SYSTEMS

The essential elements of a global information system are in Figure 1. At the boundary of the system are *data inputs*. These are environmental scanning sub-systems for external environmental systems and internal monitoring. The global information system is to draw routinely on these data sources to feed the system's database. Therefore, it is necessary to identify sources of environmental scanning data and to define the processes and procedures to capture, transmit, and use the system's database.

The second set of global information system elements are *operational components*. Several types are defined. *System controls* are subsystems that maintain system and data integrity, security access, internal operations checks, and general administrative activities for the proper functioning of the system.

A second type of operational component is the *database management system*. This includes expanding and evolving data files, and the data dictionary that defines the elements of the data files and their locations, and the variables including their types, formats, locations, characteristics and meanings. Data integrity subsystems includes subsystems for bringing new data into the database (i.e., linking to environmental data sources either electronically or through direct keyboard entry), purging needed data, and assuring that data included in the database meet the data dictionary definitions. The data access subsystem provides managers with access to the needed data items under the guidance of the appropriate system security controls.

Thirdly, *user interface systems* provides access to data and analytical tools. The design of these systems is crucial to users' acceptance of the system. Ideally, a common graphical user interface would be developed for most applications and implemented using icon symbols that would be acceptable and meaningful across cultures. This is substantially the philosophy that guided the development of the Apple Macintosh and the Microsoft Windows user interfaces. Such interfaces speed the user's learning curve for the basic system and because the interface is common across most applications, it is easier for users to learn new application programs. Cross-cultural icons may increase system acceptability in diverse cultures.

Last, a set of *applications systems* are needed to provide managers *with inquiry and analysis* capabilities. Inquiry systems allow managers to monitor product sales, promotional programs, environmental trends, and other issues. Essentially, inquiry systems allow managers to obtain answers to questions of "what is?" or "what has happened in the past?" These are different from analytical questions that ask "Why?" Both types of systems are needed. Because managers will need to monitor trends in different countries, compare trends in product lines, compare sales of different distribution channels, and so forth for a plethora of questions that cannot be completely anticipated, it

FIGURE 1. Fundamental Global Information System Components

Environmental Scanning Inputs → **Database and System Operations** → **Possible Application Outputs**

Environmental Scanning Inputs

Internal Organizational Inputs

- Transaction Processing System
- Shipping Records
- Customer Database
- Sales Commissions
- Telemarketing Database
- Customer Service
- Accounts Receivables
- Pricing Standards
- Inventory Records
- Etc.

External Environmental Inputs

- Ad Hoc Market Research Studies
- Third Party Subscription Data
- On-Line Environmental Data
  - Industry Trends
  - Economic Trends
  - Advertising Costs
  - Regulatory Trends
  - Competitor Trends
  - Supply Trends
  - Scanner Data
  - Single Source Data
- Inter-Organizational Data Sharing (Business Partners)

Database and System Operations

System Internal Controls

- Database Management Systems & Controls
- Data Files
- Data Dictionary
- Data Administrator
  - Data Integrity
  - Data Access
- Data Communications

User Interface Systems

- Access Controls
- User Interfaces
- Ergonomics

Applications Systems

- Fixed Reports
- Ad Hoc Inquiries
- Statistical Analyses
- Simulation Models
- Expert Systems
- Qualitative Analyses
- Forecasting Systems

Reporting Systems

- Text Processing
- Graphics Output
  - Slides and Viewgraphs
- Electronic Output

Possible Application Outputs

Product Management

- Sales Summaries
  - Tactical Plans
  - Forecasts
- Budgets
- Profit Analyses

Communications

- Budgets
- Simulations
- Media Plans
- Impact Reports

Sales Management

- Territory Design
- Sales Forecasts
- Quota Planning
- Territory Analysis
- Channel Assessment
- Commission Reviews
  - Cost Reviews

Senior Management

- Simulate Strategy
- Financial Modeling
- Market Assessments
- Ad Hoc Reviews

will be desirable to provide relational capabilities in the design to the databases so that managers can have maximum flexibility in their inquiries. However, given the potential size of the global information system database system, and the importance of speed to users engaged in interactive inquiries, it may be necessary to balance flexibility and system responsiveness and to develop innovative approaches to inquiries. Managers will also require a diverse set of analytical decision support tools. Certainly, statistical processing tools with tables, regression, and similar capabilities will be required, but much more advanced analytical tools may also be needed as will simulation modeling, linear programming, forecasting, PERT and CPM systems. Precisely which analytical tools must be incorporated into the main global information system and which should be left to end users on networked microcomputers are questions that must be resolved in the planning stage with substantial end user input.

The fifth type of operational system in Figure 1 is *reporting systems* to provide printed and electronic output so that the results of inquiries and analysis can be preserved and displayed to other managers and incorporated in managerial reports. Such systems may involve text processing and desk top publishing, presentation and publication quality graphics, 35 millimeter slide output, and electronic microcomputer based slide shows, storyboards, computer assisted instruction, and even multinational electronic mail. Here again, it will be important to have substantial input from the intended end users because, ultimately, these systems will be the primary way by which the decision making benefits of the global information system are transmitted to other decision makers and the rest of the organization.

These environmental scanning and operational systems represent the main components of the global information system. The successful global information system will provide managers with effective information and tools to support decision making. The results may affect all managerial functions. As suggested in Figure 1, product managers can benefit through efficiently developed sales summaries, forecasts of the impacts of tactical plans, long-term product forecasts, accurate budgeting, and accurate analysis of the profit contributions of each area of the product's development program. Similarly, communications managers should be able to use the global information system to effectively simulate the impact of various promotional programs, and develop more cost-effective media plans. Sales managers may benefit by more appropriate designs of sales territories, sales forecasts (which in turn affect production costs), sales quotas for districts' and individual nations' salespersons and accounts, and so forth. The benefits of the global information system will also extend to senior managers who should be able to use the system to simulate alternative strategy decisions, develop financial models of alternative marketing strategies, more accurately assess the potentials of diverse international markets, and carry out ad hoc reviews of individual programs throughout the global reach of the organization.

An example is Teleglobe Canada which provides the communication link between Canada and all other countries in the world. In the late 1980s, Teleglobe was privatized and became regulated by the Canadian Radio and Telecommunications Commission. At the same time, the company had to report to the parent company in great detail about finance, operations, and marketing activities. Teleglobe had information architecture in place with three layers: strategic planning, management control, and operations control. Each of these layers was comprised of numerous systems, but the three layers did not interact easily among themselves. To address this issue an additional layer was developed to deal with corporate-level issues, such as profits and costs, networks and facilities, rates and tariffs (which are constantly changing), service profitability, and capital investment. Modeling capabilities also included "what-if" analysis. Ultimately, Executive Information Systems (EIS) were developed, all using the same information, but with the presentation customized to fit the needs and even the personality of each user (Comshare Exception Reporting, 1994).

Another example is the Hong Kong and Shanghai Banking Corporation. Efficient data processing is critical to the success and survival of any bank. Anytime an acquisition was made, the holding company had to convert existing information systems to match that of the parent company. This is a difficult task due to technological and cultural differences.

In the 1980s, competition became more intense due to the deregulation of banking in the United States and increased trend for free trade. Also, banks faced competition from other financial institutions such as credit companies and brokerage houses. The result was that making money on loans (interest income) became very difficult. Banks, however, have many other products such as letters of credits, credit cards, and investment management. Recognizing the opportunity, the Hong Kong Bank developed a sophisticated profitability EIS and Decision Support System (DDS). This systems monitors performance and profitability for every bank, branch, and department in the organization. In addition, profitability is tracked by product and by customer (Turban, Mclean and Wetherbe, 1996).

MANAGING THE PLANNING AND DEVELOPMENT OF THE SYSTEM

An effective global information system is a continually evolving system. Senior managers and information systems developers are advised to define the general parameters of a comprehensive, ideal system, and then to focus on initial information priorities. These priorities can then be developed within the standards established for the global information system so that future developments will have effective interfaces to the initial modules. Therefore, the initial planning stages must be guided by a clear vision of the future of the organization in global context with involvement of top level management, and senior managers in information systems.

Information systems managers cling to an orientation model that is largely national, and top down, i.e., from headquarters out to the subsidiaries (Marshall, 1996). With ever-increasing international competition, businesses must realize that to retain this orientation while attempting to compete in an international environment will hurt them strategically. Information systems development must be conceptualized as global, reflective of the global operations, to achieve strategic advantage. The issue an organization must then address is how to accelerate the information systems development cycle sufficiently to enable the company to realize a strategic advantage in the market. The corporation with the greatest ability to reduce uncertainty and deal with the increased complexity of the international competitive arena will stand the better chance of survival in the global marketplace (Ohmae, 1995; Bartlett and Ghoshal, 1991). Time is crucial. Information systems will play a significant role only if their products can be delivered fast enough to provide a strategic advantage. To survive in a global market and achieve timely information systems development, systems must be developed, for the most part, locally.

Culture and National Differences

Steinbart, P. J. & R. Nath (1992) cite the example of Phillip Morris encountering many factors that hindered its efforts in international systems development. These factors include such issues as language barriers, differing regulations, the lack of global information product vendors, inadequate facilities in foreign operations, differing accounting standards and tax codes, and cultural barriers and biases. Mannheim (1991) in a study of related issues, pointed out that other difficulties include the lack of a consistent telecommunications infrastructure, lack of support for information systems projects from top management, compilations in ensuring data security, and challenges with differing local postal, telephone, and telegraph utilities in the various countries.

Language differences are an obvious obstacle to information collection and transmission. In some cases, simple translation of words may not be sufficient, especially between languages such as Japanese and English, which do not have a common origin. Cultural attitudes toward secrecy, authority and risk taking can also influence the effectiveness of an information system. If it is culturally unacceptable for a local manager to accept criticism or policy dictates from outsiders, it will be difficult to maintain tight control over subsidiaries, no matter how well the communication system functions.

Economic aspects of the environment, such as local competition, currency fluctuation and inflation are important considerations. Variations in tax structure and in the amount of legislative control exercised over MNEs in the various host countries can also complicate information flow.

To provide the many types of business information necessary to the various levels of the organizational hierarchy, a certain amount of redundancy may have to be built into the information system. Local managers will justifiably prefer to receive planning and profitability reports in terms of local currencies and prepared in accordance with accounting principles, while top management at corporate headquarters of a Canadian multinational will want subsidiary performance data prepared in Canadian dollars. The sheer volume of information to be processed can become overwhelming to management with subsidiaries located in several countries, each with its own particular currency regulations, inflation rate, and tax system.

Europcar Interent, the largest European-based car rental agency combines 55 independent systems with various data types, many of which prior, to 1994, were incompatible. At that time, Europcar was interested in integrating its business practices, customer preferences, and related data into a single system. However, to complicate matters, the company had to simultaneously develop a uniform set of business practices, or corporate standards, to support the new single business entity. Furthermore, Europcar had to consider the variety of languages spoken in the nine countries involved as well as different currencies and cultures (Greebaym, 1994). In January of 1999, a single monetary policy will begin operation across Europe. For the next three years, national currencies will co-exist as non-decimal denominations of the Euro (the new single currency of Europe). Euro notes and coins will enter circulation in January and June of 2002. Thus, Europcar is now well positioned for the period of "virtual monetary union" and the transition to a single currency in Europe (*Financial Times*, 1998).

In addition to the quality and quantity of information to be collected and processed for management, the characteristics of the system through which this information flows must be considered. A basic issue to be resolved in the management of a multinational is the trade-off between centralization and decentralization. Foreign subsidiaries may be viewed simply as extensions of the home operations, with tight centralized control, or they may be seen as independent subunits and allowed considerable freedom.

The degree of decentralization of decision making is reflected in management attitudes toward subsidiaries and in the organizational structure that provides a framework for the information system. A balance must be achieved between corporate control and local autonomy. Management at the subsidiary level will be able to weigh the effects of local environmental conditions when making decisions, while headquarters has the advantage of a broader view of overall corporate strategy. Bartlett and Ghoshal (1991) have developed four models of organizational structure. These models are based upon, first, the pressures for global integration basically deriving from competitive pressures to reduce costs, and, secondly, the pressures for organizations to respond or adapt quickly to local needs and conditions. These organizational models are featured in Figure 2. To remain competitive, even the global and international models which feature low pressures for local responsiveness, must develop information systems that have the capacity to adapt to the new international environment.

Competitive pressures dictate that the traditional, national model of information systems development is not adequate to address this new international environment. A newer approach must emphasize greater development speed, yet, at the same time, allow for individual multinational units to conform to their local environments. To facilitate coordination between units, data must

FIGURE 2. Organizational Models for International Expansion

		Pressures for Local Responsiveness: Low	Pressures for Local Responsiveness: High
Pressures for Global Integration	**High**	GLOBAL	TRANSNATIONAL
	Low	INTERNATIONAL	MULTINATIONAL

Adopted from Bartlett and Ghoshal (1991)

INTERNATIONAL: Using existing capabilities to expand into foreign markets

MULTINATIONAL: Several subsidiaries operating as stand-alone business units in multiple countries.

GLOBAL: Views the world as a single market. Operations are controlled centrally from the corporate office.

TRANSNATIONAL: Specialized facilities permit local responsiveness. Complex coordination mechanisms provide global integration.

flow between them. Upward connectivity–allowing for overall coordination among units–must also be addressed.

DATA COLLECTION ISSUES

The adequacy of a global information system is constrained by the quality of the data on which it is able to draw. The fundamental issues related to data quality are availability, timeliness, validity, comparability, accuracy, and reliability over time, across organizations, and across national boundaries. Including erroneous data in the system may lead to inaccurate analyses and unsound business decisions, therefore, it is vital that procedures be in place to assess data quality (Rice and Mahmoud, 1984).

External environmental data can take two forms; secondary data or primary data. *Primary data* are data that are collected by the researcher for the first time for the explicit purpose at hand. Data from a survey of customers that the researcher carried out in order to assess customer satisfaction would be primary data. For example, government census reports on the population of a country are a form of secondary data when used by a manager to assess the sales potential of a country. *Secondary data* are data that were originally collected for another purpose, but are available to the researcher in some form and may be applicable to the researchers' current purpose.

International managers depend heavily on secondary data resources for most environmental monitoring activities. Frequently used data sources may include publications of the United Nations, international trade associations, host governments, and a variety of private international data subscription services (Stewart, 1984; Dialog Information Services, Inc., 1993; Czinkota and Ronkainen, 1995). Secondary data can be of great benefit to the researcher, but can present problems. The precise information needed by the researcher might not be available, and if it is available in one country, it might not be available in another. Even when the desired information is available, the secondary data may be old, having been produced several months or years earlier. For example, the United States Census is taken only once every ten years and the results may not be fully available for several years after it is taken.

The problems of validity and comparability of data are closely related. *Validity addresses whether the data measures what the researcher expects it to measure.* If, for example, a government report refers to the number of wholesalers in a country, is the government definition of a wholesaler in this report the same as would be used by the researcher? Related to validity is the problem that secondary data often do not precisely fit the issue with which the researcher is concerned or the format that the researcher desired. Sometimes, the international market researcher must "interpret" such data as is available even though he or she recognizes that the data might not precisely refer to the issue at hand. *Comparability refers to whether secondary data on a topic that are obtained from different countries or organizations are measured, computed, or reported in the same way.* Comparability may suffer because of different definitions of terms or because of different ways of measuring or reporting data. This may especially be a problem in international research because different governments may report such things as census data, business statistics, educational data, and so forth using different categories, indices, methods of calculation, and so forth. Therefore, data that are available from different countries might not be easily compared. For example, it may be difficult to compare the number of wholesalers or industrial suppliers in the United States with the number in Japan since these terms may have different meanings in these two countries. Because comparability of secondary data can be a serious problem in establishing a database for a global information system, formal procedures should be developed to adjust the data to comparable formats or to warn users of the system of discrepancies.

Accuracy and reliability of secondary data should also be of concern to the international manager (Czinkota & Ronkainen, 1995). *Accuracy refers to how precisely the measurement is carried out.* For example, a survey may produce an estimate with a large margin of error. *Reliability refers to whether the measurement and reporting technique would produce the same results each time the measure is taken if the thing being measured has not changed.* Governments and other producers of data may differ in their ability to accurately and reliably measure social, cultural, business, or economic conditions (Czinkota & Ronkainen, 1995; and Ball & McCulloch, 1995), and in some countries it may not be uncommon for reported data to be distorted for propaganda purposes. Procedures must be put in place to verify the integrity of secondary data before it is recorded as part of the global information system. One method of assessing whether reported data are accurate or reliable is to seek two or more sources. If different sources provide similar estimates, the researcher can have more confidence in the data.

Because the market researcher has greater control in the collection of primary data, many of the problems described above are less likely to occur. However, primary data collection projects in the international context may present problems as well (Czinkota, Ronkainen, and Tarrant, 1995). Differences in cultures and languages may create problems of validity and comparability because questionnaires and other data collection instruments may have to be translated into several languages (Terpstra, 1988). One way to verify that translations are accurate would be to translate the data collection instrument into a second language and then have it retranslated into the original language by another translator. The retranslated version may then be compared to the original.

Field primary data collection is more difficult in less developed nations than in developed ones. Less developed nations may not have the communications and transportation infrastructures needed to reach the intended respondents. High levels of illiteracy may create further problems in using conventional techniques to administer questionnaires or interviews (Terpstra, 1988). Response rate problems may be accentuated since large numbers of sampled respondents may not be accessible. Another problem in less developed countries may be locating sufficient numbers of skilled data collectors and clerical staff to adequately carry out the field checks and central office checks needed to prevent "non-sampling" errors such as mistakes in recording, coding data, or entering data (Czinkota, Ronkainen, and Tarrant, 1995). However, when such research is needed to provide information to the global information system database, sufficient planning, realistic funding of the project, and careful project management following sound research practices can assure high data quality.

An example of what occasionally needs to be done is the case of Peter Johns who wanted to distribute mail-order catalogs from upscale U.S. companies to consumers in Mexico. Johns suspected that there was a rich market there, waiting to be tapped. With 30 years of international marketing experience, Johns knew that instinct was not enough. But when he tried to test his theory against hard data, he ran into a blank wall. He could not find a useful marketing study for Mexico City. Census reports were not much help because, in Mexico, they stop breaking down income levels at about $35,000, and they give ranges, rather than precise numbers, on family size (*Wall Street Journal*, 1991).

So Johns embarked on some primary research; he went into some affluent neighborhoods and found just what he had suspected: satellite dishes, imported sports cars, women carrying expensive handbags. Having decided that there was, indeed, a market for upscale catalogs in Mexico City, Johns needed mailing lists. He couldn't obtain the kind he needed. So he started to build his own lists. He asked local investors for membership lists of the city's exclusive golf clubs. He obtained directories of the parents of students at some of the city's exclusive private schools. Out of necessity, Johns was engaging in what he called "grass-root marketing intelligence" (*Wall Street Journal*, 1991).

TECHNOLOGICAL ISSUES FOR INTERNATIONAL DATA FLOWS

Even when the developers of the global information system have the assistance of the various country managers and have arranged for capturing internal and external information needed by the global information system, the information must be transmitted to the home office and to other country offices directly. This brings us to the third set of generic challenges in developing a global information system, transborder data flows. Transborder data flows, or TDF, refers to the movement of data across national boundaries. TDFs may be problematic in at least three ways: (1) technological communications problems; (2) cost issues related to host country PTT charges (postal, telegraph, and telephone agencies); and (3) host country and international regulations.

Deans and Kane (1992) have provided an excellent overview of the diverse political, legal, technological and historical issues that underlie the current status of TDFs. They note that the term "transborder data flow" is used in narrow and broad ways (1992). In the narrow definition, the term refers to data that are explicitly stored and transmitted via computer. The broader definition considers a TDF to be all data and information that cross a national border in any way or form. Although the narrow view is most often used, the broader view is gaining acceptance with the spread of various electronic technologies (Deans and Kane, 1992). For this reason, global information system developers should consider the broad definition when assessing the issues that may affect the transmission of data to the home office and the global sharing of global information system data among managers in different countries.

From a technological standpoint, the global information system developer must be concerned with whether the computer and related data collection and transmission operations in a country's local domestic office are adequate for effective transmission at reasonable speed and whether the transmission form will be acceptable to the host system in the home office. When the MNC has full control over both the home computing systems and the remote systems, this may not be problematic. However, some countries may require that computers used locally must have been produced locally (i.e., Brazil restricts the use of foreign computing equipment) (Deans and Kane, 1992). Moreover, local transmission systems regulated by the domestic "postal, telephone, and telegraph agency might not provide adequate transmission quality to allow high speed transmission, or lines might not be available for extended periods at the time that the data are to be transmitted. In general, however, technological problems can be solved, although perhaps at the cost of reducing the amount of data transmitted or some loss in the timeliness of the data.

The costs of TDF may be substantially higher than internal communications for several reasons. These include requirements that locally-produced data processing equipment be used, high tariffs on international communications and on data transmission in particular, possible taxes on data, or excessive charges for data lines (Deans and Kane, 1992). Typically, these costs should not be completely allocated to the global information system since some costs will be incurred simply to maintain the domestic operation. However, where special data lines are needed, or where tariffs or taxes specifically target data, the global information system planners will have to weigh the benefits of elaborate and timely global information system data against the incremental costs of transmission. Careful planning of the global information system data requirements, and the aggregation level of the desired data can help to limit costs so that these may not be a significant issue. Still, the cost of TDFs should be considered in the global information system planning process.

Perhaps the most significant issues faced by MNCs developing or operating international information systems will be domestic laws and regulations that may limit the types and volume of data that can be transmitted (Deans and Kane, 1992) due to concerns over privacy rights of citizens or concerns over national security or sovereignty. These issues may be as serious in developed countries as in developing or less developed countries. Over thirty nations already have laws affecting TDFs and many others are considering regulations. These include such developed nations as France (The Data Processing, Data Files, and Individual Liberties Act) and Sweden (the Data Act of 1973). Differences in laws among host countries further complicate matters. Even when laws governing TDFs are not in place, MNCs may encounter problems with government officials for exporting economic information that might be considered commonplace in a western society such as the United States but may be deemed politically sensitive elsewhere. Even in western societies, pressures may build for restrictions on the flows of market-related information as the strategic value of information is recognized. Deans and Kane (1992) note such pressures in Canada and France.

CONCLUSION: A LOCAL APPROACH TO INFORMATION DEVELOPMENT

Global firms, wishing to improve systems development decisions and practice, are challenged to accommodate pressures posed on global managers by the global contexts' variety, complexity, and unfamiliarity. Developing a cadre of global managers calls for the upgrading of the firm's personnel functions. Firms competing across borders are only as transnational as their managers and their resource policies (Adler and Bartholomew, 1992). Global management is a frame of mind, not a particular organization design (Bartlett and Ghoshal, 1991). This holds implications both for recruiting and training systems developers and managers.

A local approach to information system development is a more flexible approach. Gensler and Chou (1991) have developed four steps for a systematic global information system planning process. These steps begin with the premise that the development of global information systems should happen at the local sites and radiate outward to the whole, not start at one central location in the whole and diffuse downward. The actual development of the system should occur at the local site, using local content and information products. With some preplanning in the approach to development organization-wide, coordination and upward connectivity to the rest of the information infrastructure within the organization would not be difficult to resolve, given that certain requirements and standards are imposed upon organizational units at the outset of any development. This preplanning should ensure system conformity that will facilitate data flows yet allow compliance with local standards and technology. Facilities in different locations should be able to develop autonomous, yet cohesive, systems faster than a single, concerted development project. The key to this development process is to allow for some standardization initially, then delegate the actual development to the personnel at the sites where the systems will be used.

First, the organization must identify critical data elements. This is more of a minimum standard that must be present to make a system connectable from site to site. Second, once the data elements have been identified, the organization must standardize the format in which the data will be stored or transmitted. This refers to the size and characteristics of the data down to the lowest element level. Standardization will ensure that when data do need to flow transborder, they will already be in a format that will remain constant across organizational units in the data base, file, and record formats. This resolves the issues of interface and connectivity. Third, to maximize the probability of connectivity among the individual sites, choices of hardware and software must be limited. All units must choose among a set of previously approved hardware and software products, which will allow for future connectivity as well as local autonomy. Fourth and last, whenever possible, provide training to the appropriate personnel at the local sites, and distribute the most current information technology as widely as possible. With declining costs of information technology, hardware may be pushed lower into the organization. Teams of local information systems personnel familiar with the local environments are able to utilize newer software productivity tools to develop systems faster than a larger team working at a central site.

REFERENCES

Bartlett and Ghoshal (1991). *Transnational Management.* Homewood, IL: Richard D. Irwin Publishers.

Bidgoli, H. (1997). *Modern Information Systems for Managers.* San Diego: Academic Press, A Division of Harcourt Brace & Co.

Bryan, L. & D. Farrell (1996). *Market Unbound: Unleashing Global Capitalism.* John J. Wiley & Sons. New York.

Comshare Exception Reporting, 1994.

Czinkota, M.R. and I.A. Ronkainen. (1995). *International Marketing*. 4th Ed. The Dryden Press, Fort Worth, TX.

Czinkota, M.R., I.A. Ronkainen and J.J. Tarrant. (1995). *The Global Marketing Imperative*. 4th Ed. NTC Business Books, Lincolnwood, ILL.

Deans, C.P. & M.J. Kane. (1992). *International Dimensions of Information Systems and Technology*. Boston: PWS-Kent Publishing Co.

Dialog Information Services, Inc. (1993). *Dialog Database Catalog, 1991*. Palo Alto, CA: Dialog Information Services, Inc.

Doz, Y.L. & C.K. Prahalad. (1984). "Patterns of the Strategic Control with Multinational Corporations." *Journal of International Business Studies*, Vol. 15 No. 2, Fall.

Financial Times, 1998. Survey on Economic and Monetary Union, March 23.

Gensler, P.J. & D.C. Chou. (1991). Managing Global Information Systems. *Information Executive*. Fall.

Greebaym, J. (1994). " A Bumpy Road for Europcar." *Information Week*, February 7.

Marshall, Kimball P. (1996). *Marketing Information Systems*. Boyde & Fraser Publishing Co., Danvers, MA

Little, L.D.C. (1979). "Decision Support Systems for Marketing Managers." *Journal of Marketing*, Vol. 43 (Summer), pp. 9-26.

Little, L.D.C. (1990). "Operations Research in Industry: New Opportunities in a Changing World." The 1990 Philip McCord Morse Lecture, ORSA/TIMS Joint Meeting. Philadelphia: ORSA/Times (Oct. 29).

Mannheim, M.L. (1991). Global Information Technology: Issues & Opportunities. Proceedings of the 24th AHICSS, 172-181.

Ohmae, K. (1995). *The End of the Nation State: The Rise of Regional Economies*. New York: The Free Press.

Ramachandran, K. (1991). "Data Collection for Management Research in Developing Countries," in *The Management Research Handbook*, (eds.), N.C. Smith and P. Dainty. London: Routledge.

Rice, G. and E. Mahmoud. (1984). "Forecasting and Data Bases in International Business." *Management International Review* 24, (Fourth Quarter) pp. 59-70.

Stewart, D.W. (1984). *Secondary Research: Information Sources and Methods*. Newbury Park, CA: Sage Publications.

Steinbart, P.J & R. Nath. (1992). Problems & Issues in the Management of International Data Communications Networks: The Experience of American Companies. *MIS Quarterly*, March.

Turban, V. McLean and Wetherbe. (1996). *Information Systems for Managers*. New York: John J. Wiley & Sons.

Terpstra, V. and Ken David. (1991). *The Cultural Environment of International Business*. Cincinnati, OH: South Western Publishing Co.

Wall Street Journal, October 24, 1991.

International and Domestic Students' Perception of Library Personnel and Resources: Explaining and Predicting the Differences

Harry A. Harmon
Barbara A. Wales

SUMMARY. International students represent an increasingly important group in American higher education. Multiculturalism is valued, and institutions seek to attract a more diverse student and faculty population. Certainly this is important to university libraries as they seek to enhance the educational opportunities and experiences of all students. This manuscript employs a large sample of domestic (i.e., non-international) students and a large sample of international students to examine the research question: Does the country of origin influence the student's perception of library personnel, or their utilization of library resources? Statistical analyses reveal that the two student groups do differ along several dimensions, but are quite similar in other regards. Regression analysis is employed to predict when each group is more likely to seek help when having trouble in the library, and to predict the student's perception of helpful and polite library personnel. Analysis of variance reveals differences within the groups

Harry A. Harmon is Associate Professor of Marketing, Central Missouri State University, Dockery 200, Warrensburg, MO 64093 (E-mail: harmon@cmsu1.cmsu.edu). Barbara A. Wales is Reference Librarian and Education Psychology Bibliographer, Central Missouri State University.

[Haworth co-indexing entry note]: "International and Domestic Students' Perception of Library Personnel and Resources: Explaining and Predicting the Differences." Harmon, Harry A. and Barbara A. Wales. Co-published simultaneously in *Journal of Teaching in International Business* (The International Business Press, an imprint of The Haworth Press, Inc.) Vol. 10, No. 3/4, 1999, pp. 129-148; and: *Teaching and Program Variations in International Business* (ed: Erdener Kaynak and John R. Schermerhorn, Jr.) The International Business Press, an imprint of The Haworth Press, Inc., 1999, pp. 129-148. Single or multiple copies of this article are available for a fee from The Haworth Document Delivery Service [1-800-342-9678, 9:00 a.m. - 5:00 p.m. (EST). E-mail address: getinfo@haworthpressinc.com].

when the groups are distinguished by the frequency that each makes use of the library resources. The research extends the literature and offers insights into understanding the differences posed by the research question. Implications for library administration are offered, as are suggestions for future research. *[Article copies available for a fee from The Haworth Document Delivery Service: 1-800-342-9678. E-mail address: getinfo@haworthpressinc.com <Website: http://www.haworthpressinc.com>]*

International students represent an increasingly important group in American higher education. Multiculturalism is valued, and institutions seek to attract a more diverse student and faculty population. In 1993-94, there were 449,704 international students enrolled in institutions of higher education in the United States. Data from the National Center for Education Statistics (1995) provides statistics for comparisons. These statistics reveal that the number of international students enrolled in U.S. colleges and universities has grown steadily in the 1980s and 1990s. For example, in academic year 1980-81, 311,880 foreign students were enrolled in American colleges and universities; this figure grew to 386,850 in 1989-90, and to the latest figure of almost 450,000. While this pattern may be most evident at major universities, many smaller regional institutions are also experiencing this trend.

Most college students find that transition to the academic environment requires an adjustment period. In the past, the understanding of this transition focused on the traditional, 18-year-old college freshman progressing from high school to college. Increasingly, institutions of higher learning are seeing student populations who do not fit this stereotypical new student; the most glaring examples are non-traditional students and international students. Non-traditional students, especially older students, working adults, and women with children, significantly impact the makeup of an institution's student population (Hammond 1994). They may experience different pressures and conflicts than traditional students. Similarly, international students face unique challenges in their pursuit of higher education in a foreign country, in which cultural and language barriers abound. According to Gilton (p. 55, 1994), the phenomena of culture shock takes place ". . . when a person in a new culture finds that the unwritten rules that worked at home no longer work." Zimmermann (1995) explored intercultural communication and adaptation of international students studying at an American campus. Frequently universities with a large, diverse student population will have an international programs office (or similar office), as a campus agency to coordinate culturization and guidance efforts for the international student population. Most universities recognize the importance of providing support to this diverse group of students.

The effective use of library resources is critical to the academic success of all students (including international students), especially those enrolled in graduate programs. There is a history of assessment activities in many libraries, some specifically geared to the international student population. Focus groups, casual discussions of a small group of participants, offer a relaxed atmosphere in which to explore people's (e.g., international students') thoughts and preferences. Duffey (1996) suggests that they are especially adaptable to library settings, and several sources are available detailing the technique specifically for the library setting (Wagner and Mahmoodi, 1994).

Natowitz (1995) conducted a review of the literature concerning international students' use of U. S. academic libraries. His treatment of common issues and concerns, along with proposed solutions, provides an excellent overview of the topic. Liu (1993) noted that, at one time, a large segment of international students came from European countries. However, many international students now come from countries which do not share a common cultural heritage with the United States, which exacerbates the problems these students face. Macdonald and Sarkodie-Mensah (1988) pointed out that many international students are accustomed to a very different educational system in which lecture and rote memory play a greater part than in the U. S. system, which values analyzing and critical thinking. Libraries in the U.S. may differ significantly from the libraries international students know. For example, international students may be unfamiliar with open stacks, the classification system, and the prevalence of electronic sources.

To better explain the differences between domestic students and international students, the research reported here addressed several key issues facing library administrators. These issues include the need to assess international students' library use pattern, the frequency of use (and the understanding) of various services, and the helpfulness of library personnel. The following research question is examined in this exploratory research:

> Research Question: Does the country of origin (i.e., domestic or international) influence the student's perception of library personnel, or their utilization of library resources?

METHODOLOGY

A mail survey was employed to assess users' perceptions of the library. The literature available includes surveys that were administered to individuals using the library, either upon leaving the building or at a service point. While these efforts are helpful, a methodological shortcoming is that this technique allows input only from those individuals using the library at that narrowly defined point in time. The data collection activity reported here was designed to reach both library users and non-users. Mangione (1995) noted that an important advantage of mail surveys is the provision for large numbers of respondents to be surveyed in a relatively short period. Other advantages include the privacy permitted respondents and the dependence on visual input rather than merely auditory–a significant factor when the respondents do not share a common first language.

The questionnaire was developed from the available literature (Hao, 1992; Allen, 1993), as well as from focus groups conducted with different student groups. Several pretests were accomplished, and resulted in a final measurement instrument that differed considerably from previous research efforts. The questionnaire was designed to gather information not currently available in the literature from our two distinct sample groups. Although our primary intention was to explore the international student's library experiences, we wanted to examine this group in relation to other students rather than in isolation. Therefore, we used two sample groups, international students and "non-international," or domestic students.

The pretests suggested some minor changes were needed to satisfy a concern to eliminate, or alleviate, the language barrier as much as possible. Designing a survey to be used by individuals of varied language and ethnic backgrounds is especially challenging. Padilla and Medina (1996) cautioned that researchers need to be cognizant of many issues in multicultural assessment. Individuals of different cultural or linguistic groups often find instruments confusing or frustrating due to the cultural or language knowledge assumed.

A second, companion questionnaire was developed because we wanted to compare the international student responses to a group representative of the domestic student population. This corollary questionnaire excluded three questions which were addressed specifically to the international students. These questions were altered and disguised so that they would be appropriate for domestic students.

The international student survey was distributed through an on-campus office that serves the international student population. The instrument was mailed to all currently-enrolled international students, 463 total. The domestic student questionnaire was mailed to 600 non-international students. The university provided a random list of full-time students, that was stratified by college, academic level (undergraduate or graduate), and excluded international students. Both questionnaires were accompanied by a cover letter which explained the goals of the survey and the return procedure designed to assure participants of confidentiality. Three reminders, which frequently result in an improved response rate (Rea and Parker, 1992), were processed.

Although the mailing lists were generated by the university, they were not screened prior to mailing to verify current enrollment or addresses. These defining criteria (Churchill, 1991) for sample selection resulted in a number of ineligible potential respondents. We received 174 responses from international students; 24 surveys were undeliverable, for a response rate of 42.8%. We received 209 responses from the non-international, i.e., domestic, student group, with 15 undeliverable, for a response rate of 37.3%. Table 1 presents the calculations for the two sample groups.

The response rate, although it is satisfactory and does not compromise the value of the research, does present the chance for bias arising from nonresponse error, a potential threat to internal validity (Armstrong and Overton, 1977). We, therefore, conducted an analysis of early versus late respondents. The sample was divided into fourths based on the timing of responses (earlier versus later). No statistically significant differences were found between the first and fourth groups with regard to several questions or various demographic variables. This finding suggests that the response rate is satisfactory and that the results reported may be generalized to a larger population.

Survey results were tabulated and statistical analysis performed using SPSS. The sample was characterized by a wide range of responses within several variables. Fifty-six percent of the international students were male and 44% were female. Of the domestic students, 44% were male, and 56% female. The next section reports the preliminary findings in a generalized

TABLE 1. Response Rate Formula

CQ = Completed Questionnaires NC = Not Completed or Refused IN = Ineligible		
Response Rate Calculation Formula $$\frac{CQ}{CQ + [(CQ/CQ + IN)]\,[NC]}$$		
	Domestic	International
CQ	209	174
NC	376	265
IN	15	24
Calculated Response Rate	37.3%	42.8%

manner. The complete findings, including demographic information and frequencies, are available from the authors.

PRELIMINARY FINDINGS

International students utilize the library more frequently for all purposes than do domestic students. For example, while 41% of the international student group use the library for class assignments one to five times a week, only 31% of U.S. students do so; and 59% of the international students use the library as a place to study, versus 32% of the domestic students. These findings strengthen the importance of identifying the unique needs and problems of the international student group. The results indicate that both groups always or usually ask for help 48% of the time when they have trouble using the library. The reasons for not requesting assistance, which are discussed in a later section of the research reported here, indicate minimal difference in responses of the two groups.

CORRELATION ANALYSIS

Correlation analysis, a measure of the linear association between two variables, is frequently used in conjunction with regression analysis (Johnson and Wichern, 1988). The initial data analysis was correlation analysis. While only summarized results are presented here, the complete results are available from the authors. The more frequently domestic students use the library for research, and for class assignments, the more frequently they ask for help when they experience trouble ($r = .13$, $p < .05$; $r = .14$, $p < .04$, respectively). The same correlations are not statistically significant for the international student group. A negative correlation is reported between use of the library as a place to study, and helpful and polite library personnel, from the international students' perspective ($r = -.20$, $p < .01$); whereas domestic students report a positive correlation ($r = .13$, $p < .07$). The more students ask for help, the more helpful and polite they find the staff was statistically significant in both student groups (international $r = .30$, $p < .00$; domestic $r = .24$, $p < .00$). A series of questions asked the respondent to rate the importance of various types of holdings or services in the library. Another series of questions addressed the ease of using certain library resources. The correlation analysis of these data are not discussed here, but the relationships are discussed in a later section.

The correlation analysis suggests that there are several similarities between the two groups, a report that should be encouraging to librarians. The research reported here seeks to explain some of the variance in the responses, and to predict the phenomena indicated by the correlation matrix. An investigation of the Research Question and interpretation of the results will provide library administrators with useful information for improving weak areas, and for maximizing service to diverse clientele.

PURPOSE

The research streams reported in the literature review indicated that the country of origin impacts the student's perception of university library personnel, and influences the student's use of the facilities and resources available at a university library. Although the results reported in the literature offer insights for library administrators, those findings, as well as our preliminary analysis, suggest that there are other concerns that should be examined in additional research. Our purpose is to examine the area of interest previously suggested by the research question:

> Research Question: Does the country of origin (i.e., domestic or international) influence the student's perception of library personnel, or the utilization of library resources?

REGRESSION ANALYSIS

Recall that the correlation analysis indicated that relationships do exist between the variables of interest and the different student groups. These relationships include the perception that library personnel are helpful and polite when the student seeks help. To further investigate that relationship, a multiple regression with each of the two separate groups was performed to identify which variables predicted the student's propensity to ask for help, and which variables predicted the perception of helpful and polite library personnel.

The first regression employed ". . . how often you ask for help when having trouble using the library" as the dependent variable. A five-point Likert scale was anchored with "always" (5) and "never" (1) so that a larger number indicated the respondent more frequently asked for help. The use of this item as a dependent variable is based on the rationale that individuals use the library for different reasons. Those reasons can provide different challenges, and levels of challenge, to different individuals. A situation that is difficult or challenging to a domestic student may be less challenging to an international student, or vice versa. These situations, therefore, influence the student to seek help with overcoming the problem. This dependent variable was first regressed on a group of questions that asked how often the respondent used the library. The focus group technique is useful for exploring a research question or further defining a problem. Information gleaned from focus group interviews conducted with several different student groups suggested the following items as likely summary reasons for using the library facilities: research, class assignments, reading for fun, a place to study, library computer lab, and a place to meet friends. Although there were other reasons expressed in lesser degree by the focus group participants, the students generally agreed with the reasons that were later collapsed into these categories. The focus group technique is useful for exploring a research question or further defining a problem. Those reasons were then incorporated into the questionnaire with a response scale that ranged from "never" to "1 to 5 times a week." The regressions further clarify the preliminary correlation analysis, i.e., that the student seeks help in response to a situation. Or stated differently, the student has a reason for being in the library and impediments to the efficacy of fulfilling that purpose are to be avoided. These items are identified as *Frequency*. The results (i.e., regression significance level, the significant standardized beta coefficients, and the coefficient of determination) are reported in Table 2.

The next regression function also used ". . . how often you ask for help when having trouble using the library" as the dependent variable. The following items were the independent predictor variables: "how important is it to you that the library provide the following: scholarly journals, U.S. newspa-

TABLE 2. Dependent Variable: How Often You Ask for Help when Having Trouble Using the Library

Independent Variables: How often do you use the library for the following: ***Frequency***	Domestic	International
Research	ns	ns
Class assignments	.131	ns
Reading for fun	ns	ns
A place to study	ns	ns
Library computer lab	ns	ns
A place to meet friends	ns	ns
Regression	R^2 2%; F = 3.31; p = .071	ns

pers, popular books and magazines, magazines/newspapers from my home country and language, e-mail access, and Internet access." These items are identified as *Resources*. The response scale ranged from "not important" to "very important." The results are reported in Table 3.

The third regression with ". . . how often you ask for help when having trouble using the library" as the dependent variable was predicted by 5 independent variables that asked the respondent to "rate the ease of use for: LUIS (the online catalog), Library of Congress Classification System, CD-ROM Indexes for Journals and Magazines, Print Indexes for Journals and Magazines, and World Wide Web." These items are identified as *Utility*. The response scale ranged from "very difficult" (1) to "very easy" (4). The respondent could also select "don't know" which was then coded zero. These regression results are reported in Table 4.

Another series of regressions employed the dependent variable "when you ask for help, have you found that library personnel are helpful and polite." The three sets of independent variables described in the preceding sections, *Frequency, Resources,* and *Utility,* were again used to predict the outcome, i.e., did you find the library personnel helpful and polite when you asked for help. These results are reported in Tables 5, 6, and 7.

MANOVA ANALYSIS

Our next analysis was to determine if the volume of library use, or the frequency of library visits, impacts the student's perception of library person-

TABLE 3. Dependent Variable: How Often You Ask for Help When Having Trouble Using the Library

Independent Variables: How important is it to you that the library provide the following: ***Frequency***	Domestic	International
Scholarly journals	ns	ns
U. S. newspapers	ns	ns
Popular books and magazines	ns	ns
Magazines/ newspapers from my home country & language	ns	ns
E-mail access	ns	ns
Internet access	ns	ns
Regression	ns	ns

TABLE 4. Dependent Variable: How Often You Ask for Help When Having Trouble Using the Library

Independent Variable: Rate the following on ease of use: ***Utility***	Domestic	International
LUIS, our online catalog	ns	.143
Library of Congress Classification System	ns	ns
CD-ROM Indexes for Journals and Magazines	ns	ns
Print Indexes for Journals and Magazines	ns	ns
World Wide Web	ns	ns
Regression	ns	R^2 2%; F = 3.52; p = .062

TABLE 5. Dependent Variable: When You Ask for Help, Have You Found That Library Personnel Are Helpful and Polite

Independent Variable: How often do you use the library for the following: ***Frequency***	Domestic	International
Research	ns	.ns
Class assignments	.179	ns
Reading for fun	ns	ns
A place to study	ns	−.279
Library computer lab	ns	ns
A place to meet friends	ns	.165
Regression	R^2 3%; F = 6.18; p = .014	R^2 5%; F = 4.81; p = .009

nel. The analysis also examined if the frequency of use influenced the degree of importance the student attached to various library resources. We performed a series of multiple analysis of variance (MANOVA) to accomplish this purpose. This technique is useful for examining the relationship between a combination of two (or more) dependent response metrically-scaled measures, and a set of nonmetric predictor variables. The first requirement to

TABLE 6. Dependent Variable: When You Ask for Help Have You Found That Library Personnel Are Helpful and Polite

Independent Variable: How important is it to you that the library provide the following: ***Resources***	Domestic	International
Scholarly journals	ns	ns
U. S. newspapers	.190	ns
Popular books and magazines	ns	ns
Magazines/ newspapers from my home country & language	ns	ns
E-mail access	ns	ns
Internet access	.211	ns
Regression	R^2 4%; F = 5.36; p = .005	ns

TABLE 7. Dependent Variable: When You Ask for Help, Have You Found That Library Personnel Are Helpful and Polite

Independent Variable: Rate the following on ease of use: ***Utility***	Domestic	International
LUIS, our online catalog	ns	.129
Library of Congress Classification System	.52	ns
CD-ROM Indexes for Journals and Magazines	ns	ns
Print Indexes for Journals and Magazines	ns	−.158
World Wide Web	ns	ns
Regression	R^2 2%; F = 4.81; p = .029	R^2 3%; F = 3.02; p = .051

satisfy before any meaningful research to examine this aspect of the research question is to establish a satisfactory measure of the frequency that the library is used or visited. This measure would indicate the number of times the facility was visited for multiple reasons. Recall that our measurement instrument indicates the respondent's assessment of library personnel, and the respondent's self-reported frequency of using the library's resources. The initial analysis computed a summary *Frequency* measure, the mean of six items. These six items (as detailed in a previous section) described how often the student used the library for research, class assignments, reading for fun, a place to study, computer lab, and a place to meet friends. Because the *Frequency* scale had not been employed in previous research, nor was a similar scale available in the literature, the reliability of the measurement scale was examined. We first examined the coefficient alpha, and then the item-to-total correlations (Cronbach, 1951). Acceptable coefficient alpha, .74 (Nunnally, 1952), and satisfactory item-to-total correlations are reported. The item-to-total correlations are low, which suggests that redundancy within the items is not a problem (Singh, 1991).

Multivariate normality, critical in multivariate data analysis (Hair et al., 1992), frequently inflates the chi-square if the assumption is violated. We next performed a Q-Q plot analysis (Johnson and Wichern, 1988) to determine if the errors appear to be normally distributed and concluded that the data did not violate this assumption. We then proceeded to examine the research question by splitting the two samples at the median Frequency score, and labeled the halves "Low Frequency" and "High Frequency." These predictor groups were the basis for a MANOVA to determine if the frequency of library use impacted the respondent's perception of library personnel, or the adequacy of library resources. Or, is there a statistically significant difference in the perception of the Low Frequency group versus the High Frequency group? The ANOVA/MANOVA results, summarized and presented in Tables 8, 9, and 10, are discussed in the next section, as are the implications drawn from the regression analysis.

DISCUSSION AND IMPLICATIONS

The regression function that describes *how often you ask for help when having trouble using the library* indicates that domestic students who are working on class assignments seek help (Table 2), while the difficulty in

TABLE 8. ANOVA International Students: How Often You Ask for Help When Having Trouble Using the Library?

Means	
Low Frequency	**High Frequency**
3.545	3.306
F approx = 3.289; prob > F = .071	

TABLE 9. MANOVA for Domestic Students' Use of Library on the Importance of Resources

How important is it to you that the library provide the following?	F value	Means(c)	
		Low Frequency	High Frequency
Scholarly journals	7.08a	2.66	2.43
U.S. newspapers	5.42b	2.63	2.42
Popular books and magazines	6.19b	2.73	2.54
Magazines/newspapers from my home country	7.98a	1.94	1.62
E-mail access	13.28a	2.69	2.36
Internet access	9.15a	1.22	1.48

F approximation = 3.59, MANOVA Wilks' criterion prob > F = .002
(a) significant at 0.01 level
(b) significant at .05 level
(c) 3 = very important; 1 = not important

TABLE 10. MANOVA for Domestic Students' Ease of Use of Library Resources

Rate the following on ease of use:	F value	Means(c)	
		Low Frequency	High Frequency
LUIS, our online catalog	3.40b	3.27	3.03
Library of Congress Classification System	1.68	2.04	1.78
Print indexes for journals and magazines	0.45	2.36	2.48
CD-ROM Indexes for journals and magazines	3.59b	2.86	2.52
World Wide Web	0.45	1.94	1.62

F approximation = 1.82, MANOVA Wilks' criterion prob > F = .11
(a) significant at .01 level
(b) significant at .05 level
(c) after recording: 4 = very difficult; 1 = very easy

using LUIS (the online catalog system) predicts when international students seek help (Table 4). These findings are interesting in what does not predict the student's asking for help. When international students use the library for any of the six reasons provided (the *Frequency* measures), they do not seek help. Although this finding might be encouraging, it may provide misleading information. For example, could the finding indicate that international students are precluded from seeking help for some unknown, covert reason, although they need help? However, this finding might be tempered by other findings with international students. We report that the ease of using LUIS is statistically significant with asking for help, which seems to indicate a willingness to seek help, at least for this area of difficulty. The findings in Table 2 also indicate that the frequency of visits does not drive the students' request for help. That is, the infrequent visitor is as likely as the frequent visitor to seek help for a problem. Furthermore, if frequency is a proxy for quantity or volume of time spent in the library, the results are likewise encouraging. It is not simply familiarity with the surroundings and personnel that encourages requests for assistance.

The lack of significant findings reported in Table 3 is encouraging. Resources that are important to students are no more likely to cause students to ask for help than are the less important resources. The non-significant findings could indicate that students do not treat these resources as important. However, the frequencies reported in Table 11 indicate that most of the *Resources* items are very important or somewhat important to both student groups. Of course, the reported level of importance is not necessarily a proxy for "how frequently do you use" the resource.

A perception of helpful and polite library personnel by domestic students is predicted by the need to work on class assignments (Table 5), by the importance attached to the availability of U.S. newspapers (Table 6), by the importance attached to Internet access (Table 6), and by the ease in using the Library of Congress Classification System (Table 7). These results are meaningful and indicate the importance of maintaining easy-to-use resources, and the need for library personnel to be available to assist students. The implications include the library's need to be informed about traditional resource needs (e.g., newspapers), and current technology resources (e.g., Internet). The need to be a helpful and polite librarian would seem to be a daunting task for contemporary personnel. Domestic students equate the same degree of importance to helpful and polite personnel for a class assignment as they do for Internet questions. Student inquiries in these areas would seem to be quite different and require diverse expertise by the library personnel. Is it realistic to expect personnel to be knowledgeable in all areas, or should personnel be assigned areas in which they can demonstrate expertise.

International students present different challenges for library personnel as

TABLE 11. How Important Is It to You That the Library Provide the Following?

			International	Domestic
Scholarly Journals	Not Important	%	4	7
	Somewhat Important	%	29	33
	Very Important	%	67	60
	Number of Responses		169	208
U.S. Newspapers	Not Important	%	6	8
	Somewhat Important	%	29	32
	Very Important	%	65	60
	Number of Responses		169	209
Popular Books & Magazines	Not Important	%	5	4
	Somewhat Important	%	30	29
	Very Important	%	65	67
	Number of Responses		172	208
Magazines & Newspapers from Home Country	Not Important	%	5	42
	Somewhat Important	%	30	41
	Very Important	%	65	17
	Number of Responses		169	209
E-mail Access	Not Important	%	2	10
	Somewhat Important	%	14	29
	Very Important	%	84	61
	Number of Responses		171	208
Internet Access	Not Important	%	4	8
	Somewhat Important	%	11	21
	Very Important	%	85	71
	Number of Responses		171	208

evidenced by the inverse regression relationships. This group perceives library personnel as less helpful and polite as the student experiences more difficulty with using the print indexes (−.158, Table 7). This inverse relationship could be explained by an inadequate understanding of the language. International students perceive library personnel to be less helpful and polite when the library is used as a place to study. The standardized beta coefficient (−.279) is statistically significant (Table 5). This finding may be explained by information gathered in the focus group sessions that were conducted prior to collecting the sample data. Some focus group participants reported a noise level in the library that interfered with their ability to study. The regression results may suggest that international students believe library personnel are responsible for maintaining an environment conducive to studying, from the students' perspective. Additional evidence to support that conclusion is offered by two other relationships. First, the results indicate a direct relationship between ease in using LUIS and the perception of helpful and polite library personnel (Table 7); and second, the direct relationship between meeting friends in the library and helpful and polite library personnel (Table 5). International students believe library personnel are more helpful and polite when the student experiences more difficulty in using the online catalog system. The perception of helpful and polite library personnel increases when the international student uses the library for meeting friends. Additional comments are offered in the Limitations section concerning this relationship.

These results from the international student sample offer opportunities for library administration to proactively respond to the suitability of the library as a studying environment, and encourages administration to derive benefit from the positive perception of the library for social encounters. Administrative attention might be directed to the inverse relationships reported for the difficulty experienced in using traditional resources and technological resources, and the helpfulness and politeness of the library personnel. International students perceive the library personnel as less helpful and polite when they experience difficulty with print indexes, but more so when they experience difficulty with the online catalog system. This opposite relationship may be the result of language difficulties that instruction for using the technology (perhaps more "show and tell" instruction) can overcome; whereas, print indexes might require a broader understanding of the language before instruction can ameliorate the difficulty.

The MANOVA/ANOVA results for Low Frequency group versus High Frequency group offer several statistically significant differences. The significant findings and implications are discussed for library administration consideration. International students differ in their perception of library personnel depending on the student's usage of the library. Table 8 indicates a statistically significant difference in how often the student asks for help when they are having trouble using the library. The Low Frequency group indicates that as a group, they are more likely to seek help (3.545), than is the High Frequency group (3.306). Although we might intuitively expect that to be the case, the results are encouraging in that the student who might be unfamiliar with the library demonstrates a higher tendency to seek help. Perhaps the library personnel have succeeded in creating a comfort zone for the Low Frequency user. The High Frequency user could be demonstrating more proficiency in solving problems encountered in using the library facilities, also an encouraging prospect. The ANOVA for the international students split at the median for Low and High Frequency groups and their perception that library personnel are helpful and polite was not statistically significant. This again is encouraging to library administration. International students, regardless of how often they use the library for multiple reasons, do not perceive a difference in the helpfulness and politeness of library personnel that is determined by the student's use of the library. Two MANOVA analyses, the importance of different library resources, and the ease of use of library resources, were not significant. In both instances, the frequency that international students used the library did not distinguish the *Resources* or the *Utility* measures.

The MANOVA analysis with domestic students provides insights into the perception that students have of library personnel and library facilities. The Low Frequency and the High Frequency groups of domestic students do not differ in the likelihood that they will seek help when they experience difficulty in using the library; nor in their perception of helpful and polite library personnel. The Low versus High Frequency groups do attach different levels of importance (statistically significant) to certain library resources, presented in Table 9. Although as a group they use the library less, the Low Frequency group believes these resources are more important than does the High Frequency group, except for Internet access. The High Frequency user may be indicating that these resources are the norm and the use of them is an expected reason for the library to offer the resources.

The MANOVA for domestic students' ease of use of library resources approaches statistical significance (prob > F = .11), and is therefore reported in Table 10 for non-generalizable examination. It is interesting to note that the Low Frequency group reported higher mean scores for most of the ease of use items than did the High Frequency group. This counterintuitive result might be explained by the response of library staff to students' requests for assistance. The Low Frequency student seeks more help (or first-time help) which results in the library person assisting the student one-on-one for a specific need. Conversely the High Frequency student has experience with the resources, and perhaps has had a previous demonstration by the library person relative to the situation at hand. The High Frequency student may therefore choose to work it out rather than seek help the next time (or some future times) he or she is using the library resources. The subsequent occasions become the salient experience that is recalled and reported in the data.

Summary data are presented in Table 12 that may explain why students do not ask for help when they experience trouble in using library facilities. We report frequencies for each of the six options tabulated for both low and high frequency groups for the two samples. Respondents could select multiple

TABLE 12. Frequencies: What Keeps You from Asking for Help from Library Personnel? Check All That Apply.

Reason for not requesting help . . .	Domestic Students		International Students	
	Low Frequency User	*High Frequency User*	*Low Frequency User*	*High Frequency User*
I am too embarrassed to ask for help . . .	7	10	12	8
There is not enough staff to help me . . .	18	24	3	0
I have trouble with English . . .	1	0	0	1
I do not want to bother the library workers . . .	12	17	30	7
The personnel do not seem friendly and helpful . . .	13	18	35	8
I do not always have time for help . . .	35	43	34	9

reasons for not using the library from the options provided. Therefore the numbers reported are frequencies only because percentages would be misleading and inappropriate. Library administrators may deem this information helpful in discerning the latent reasons for use/nonuse of library resources and facilities when considered in conjunction with the regression functions we report.

LIMITATIONS AND FUTURE RESEARCH NEEDS

Future research that utilizes more qualitative information would be helpful in explaining and interpreting some of these data. For example, the reason international students did not ask for help was unfriendly library personnel. While this information is important to library administration, it needs to be investigated to determine why that is the perception of the Low Frequency user but not the High Frequency user. Is that a dominant perception with all student challenges, or with only some of the challenges? Likewise a series of focus group interviews, or in-depth interviews with selected international students should examine and refine the reasons that the student experienced difficulty with print indices. We suggest that language may be the barrier but can not confirm that suggestion with the current research. Confirming or disconfirming that possibility would add considerably to strategy formulation.

REFERENCES

Allen, Mary B. (1993). "International Students in Academic Libraries: A User Survey." *College & Research Libraries* 54 (July), 323-333.

Armstrong, J. Scott and Terry S. Overton. (1977). A Estimating Nonresponse Bias in Mail Surveys." *Journal of Marketing Research* 14 (Aug), 396-402.

Churchill, Gilbert A., Jr. (1991). *Marketing Research: Methodological Foundations.* Chicago: Dryden Press, 614-618.

Cronbach, L. J. (1951). "Coefficient Alpha and the Internal Structure of Tests." *Psychometrika* 16 (October), 297-334.

Duffey, Jeanne. (1996). "Focus Groups Create Snapshots of Community Needs." *Missouri Library World* (spring): 6.

Gilton, Donna L. (1994). "A World of Difference: Preparing for Information Literacy Instruction for Diverse Groups." *Multicultural Review* 3, no. 3 (Sept), 54-55.

Hair, Joseph F., Jr., Rolph E. Anderson, Ronald L. Tatham, and William C. Black. (1992). *Multivariate Data Analysis with Readings.* New York: Macmillian Publishing Company.

Hammond, Carol. (1994). "Nontraditional Students and the Library: Opinions, Preferences, and Behaviors." *College & Research Libraries* 55 (July), 324.

Hao, Junhong. (1992). "Chinese Students' Use of a Medium-Sized American Academic Library." Master's thesis, Central Missouri State University.

Johnson, Richard A. and Dean W. Wichern. (1988). *Applied Multivariate Statistical Analysis.* Englewood Cliffs, New Jersey: Prentice Hall.

Littlejohn, Nancy, Mary Tygett, and Barbara Wales. (1994). *Assessment Design for Academic Libraries: Measuring Patron and Employee Satisfaction with Services and Operations* (ERIC ED 373 782).

Liu, Zimig. (1993). "Difficulties and Characteristics of Students from Developing Countries in Using American Libraries." *College & Research Libraries* 54 (Jan), 25-26.

Macdonald, Gina and Elizabeth Sarkodie-Mensah (1988), "ESL Students and American Libraries." *College & Research Libraries* 49 (Sept): 426.

Mangione, Thomas W. (1995). *Mail Surveys: Improving the Quality.* Thousand Oaks, California: Sage Publications, 6.

McKenzie, Darlene E. (1995). *Survey of Library and Information Needs of the International Students at Kent State University* (ERIC, ED 390 410), 34.

Moeckel, Nancy and Jenny Presnell. (1995). "Recognizing, Understanding, and Responding: "Program Model of Library Instruction Services for International Students." *The Reference Librarian* no. 51-52, 312-313.

Nance-Mitchell, Veronica E. (1996). "A Multicultural Library: Strategies for the Twenty-First Century." *College & Research Libraries* 57 (Sept), 405-413.

National Center for Education Statistics, *Digest of Education Statistics.* Washington, D C: National Center for Education Statistics, 1995, 441.

Natowitz, Allen. (1995). "International Students in U. S. Academic Libraries: Recent Concerns and Trends." *Research Strategies* 13, no. 1 (winter), 4-16.

Nunnally, Jum C. (1978). *Psychometric Theory.* New York: McGraw-Hill Book Company.

Padilla, Amado M. and Antonio Medina. (1996). "Cross-Cultural Sensitivity in Assessment: Using Tests in Culturally Appropriate Ways," in *Handbook of Multicultural Assessment: Clinical, Psychological, and Educational Applications*, ed. Lisa A. Suzuki, Paul J. Meller, and Joseph G. Ponterotto. San Francisco: Jossey-Bass Publishers, 3-28.

Rea, Louis M. and Richard A. Parker. (1992). *Designing and Conducting Survey Research: A Comprehensive Guide.* San Francisco: Jossey-Bass Publishers, 85-86.

Singh, Jagdip. (1991). "Redundancy in Constructs: Problem, Assessment, and an Illustrative Example." *Journal of Business Research* 22, 255-280.

Wagner, Mary M. and Suzanne H. Mahmoodi. (1994). *A Focus Group Interview Manual* (n.p.: American Library Association, Continuing Library Education Network and Exchange Round Table).

Westbrook, Lynn and Sharon DeDecker. (1993). "Supporting User Needs and Skills to Minimize Library Anxiety: Considerations for Academic Libraries." *The Reference Librarian* no. 40, 44.

Zimmermann, Stephanie. (1995). "Perceptions of Intercultural Communication Competence and International Student Adaptation to an American Campus." *Communication Education* 44, no. 4 (Oct), 321-35.

Index

For Product Safety Concerns and Information please contact our EU representative GPSR@taylorandfrancis.com
Taylor & Francis Verlag GmbH, Kaufingerstraße 24, 80331 München, Germany

www.ingramcontent.com/pod-product-compliance
Ingram Content Group UK Ltd.
Pitfield, Milton Keynes, MK11 3LW, UK
UKHW022032061126
477531UK00008B/290
* 9 7 8 1 1 3 8 9 9 6 7 7 9 *